AMERICAN

ACLU

HANDBOOKS FOR YOUNG AMERICANS

The Rights of Women and Girls

KARY L. MOSS

with an introduction by Norman Dorsen

PUFFIN BOOKS

This book is dedicated to my daughter, Jessa Rose

PUFFIN BOOKS
Published by the Penguin Group
Penguin Putnam Inc., 375 Hudson Street, New York, New York 10014, U.S.A.
Penguin Books Ltd, 27 Wrights Lane, London W8 5TZ, England
Penguin Books Australia Ltd, Ringwood, Victoria, Australia
Penguin Books Canada Ltd, 10 Alcorn Avenue, Toronto, Ontario, Canada M4V 3B2
Penguin Books (N.Z.) Ltd, 182-190 Wairau Road, Auckland 10, New Zealand

Penguin Books Ltd, Registered Offices: Harmondsworth, Middlesex, England

First published in the United States of America by Puffin Books,
a member of Penguin Putnam Inc., 1998

1 3 5 7 9 10 8 6 4 2

LIBRARY OF CONGRESS CATALOGING-IN-PUBLICATION DATA
Moss, Kary L.
The rights of women and girls / Kary L. Moss ; with an introduction by Norman Dorsen.
p.   cm. — (ACLU handbooks for young Americans)
Includes bibliographical references and index.
Summary: Presents a historical overview of the status of women in society and discusses
the evolution of rights for women and the relevant court decisions that made those rights
possible.
ISBN 0-14-037782-4 (pbk.)
1. Women's rights—Juvenile literature. 2. Sex role—Juvenile literature.
3. Women—Social conditions—Juvenile literature. [1. Women's rights. 2. Sex role.
3. Women—Social conditions.]
I. Dorsen, Norman. II. Title. III. Series.
HQ1236.M66 1998 305.42—dc21 97-36596 CIP AC

Printed in U.S.A.
Set in ITC Century Book

"I'm not afraid of storms, for I'm learning how to sail my ship."

—Jo, in *Little Women,* by Louisa May Alcott

CONTENTS

FOREWORD

This guide sets forth the rights of women and girls under the present law and offers suggestions on how they can be protected. It is one of a series of handbooks for young adults which is published in cooperation with the American Civil Liberties Union (ACLU).

This guide offers no assurances that the rights it discusses will be respected. The laws may change, and in some of the topics covered in these pages they change quite rapidly. An effort has been made to note those parts of the law where movement is taking place, but it is not always possible to predict accurately when the law *will* change.

Even if the laws remain the same, their interpretations by courts and administrative officials often vary. In a federal system such as ours, there is a built-in problem since state and federal law differ, not to mention the confusion between states. In addition, there are wide variations in how particular courts and administrative officials will interpret the same law at any given moment.

If you encounter what you consider to be a specific abuse of your rights, you should seek legal assistance. There are a number of agencies that may help you, among them ACLU affiliate offices, but bear in mind that the ACLU is a limited-purpose organization. In many communities, there are federally funded legal service offices which provide assistance to persons who cannot afford the costs of legal representation. In general, the rights that the ACLU defends are freedom of inquiry and expression, due process of law, equal protection of the laws, and privacy. The authors in this series discuss other rights (even though they sometimes fall outside the ACLU's usual concern) in order to provide as much guidance as possible.

These publications carry the hope that Americans, informed of their rights, will be encouraged to exercise them. Through their exercise, rights are given life. If they are rarely used, they may be forgotten and violations may become routine.

It is of special importance that young people learn what their rights are and that there is such a thing as "rights"—individual liberties that the government, no matter how strong, must honor. Only a self-confident country can remain faithful to such a vision, and young people are the future of all countries, whether or not these recognize the value of rights to a thriving civilization. The handbooks in this series are designed to contribute to this goal.

Norman Dorsen
Stokes Professor,
New York University School of Law
President, ACLU 1976–1991

PREFACE

I will never forget the time my seventh-grade math teacher yelled at me in class for getting a math problem wrong, suggesting that I made the mistake because I was a girl. I'll never forget that I was forced to take a home-economics course instead of shop in high school. There were many other instances during my childhood where I felt treated unfairly because of my gender. Fortunately, I had the support of a loving family and eventually learned that these types of events said more about society than about me personally.

Not until college, however, did I really learn that the barriers I had confronted were even more formidable than I had realized. They were embodied in all the institutions around us—schools, government, the workplace, and the media. And it was not until I went to law school that I became fully aware of the extent to which the legal system has supported discrimination. As a lawyer, I have come to appreciate the power of the law, and the many ways that it can be used positively to break down barriers, both institutional and attitudinal. The most important, and first, step is through education. It is with education in mind that I write this book.

ACKNOWLEDGMENTS

I would like to thank the following people for their assistance with this book: Donna Allen, Norman Dorsen, Angela White, and all those at Puffin Books who helped with its production. Additionally, Isabelle Katz Pinzler, Deborah Ellis, and Susan Deller Ross co-wrote, with me, *The Rights of Women*, published by Southern Illinois University Press in 1993. It was at the request of Puffin Books that I turned *The Rights of Women* into a book for teenagers. I would like to thank my coauthors for their earlier work and inspiration in this field of the law. Finally, I would like to thank Kate Bush for her invaluable comments and insights into several chapters.

1

THE LEGAL SYSTEM

What does it mean to have a legal right?

Having a legal right means that society has given a person a legally enforceable way to get help from the government, whose agencies and representatives include the courts, governmental agencies, the police, and lawyers employed by the states to help the poor who have been arrested.

The right itself is *abstract*—such as the right to privacy, the right to equal protection of the laws—but the enforcement of the right is *concrete*. For example, a woman might have a right to choose an abortion; a minority person the right to a job, free from discrimination; or a person accused of a crime the right to an attorney. Enforcing the right yields something specific: the abortion, the job, the attorney.

These legal rights entitle us to be treated fairly—in the home, school, workplace, and society. Rights entitle women to be treated the same as men, people of color the same as white people, disabled people the same as those who are able-bodied. They entitle us to receive money when we have been wrongly injured; they guarantee performance of a certain task, such as reinstatement to a job if we have been wrongly fired.

Without legal rights, we would live in a society where slavery would be acceptable; where you could be sent to prison without a fair trial; where the government could spy on you in your home, deny you the chance to practice the religion of your choice, or associate with those people you most want to be with. You could be forced to have children against your will, lose your job if you became pregnant, or barred from attending college because you are a girl.

Legal rights guarantee our freedom. They are the cornerstone of our democratic system of government. But many people in this country have had a long and difficult struggle to receive their full and appropriate legal rights.

Where do legal rights come from?

There are four main sources of law in this country.

1. The Constitution is the most important source of our rights; it is the supreme law of the land. The Constitution, which includes the Bill of Rights, is designed to prevent any one of the three branches of government—the executive (the president), Congress (our elected officials), or the judiciary (the courts)—from becoming too powerful. This document provides the building blocks upon which all other rights and protections depend.

Some of the most important rights contained in the Constitution are the right to free speech; the right to privacy; the right to not be subjected to searches of your home, body, or car; and the right to have all laws applied fairly, without regard to race or sex.

The Constitution, when created, was not perfect. It explicitly omitted from its protections two key groups: African-Americans and women. At the time of the founding fathers, as

2

the group of men who did the actual writing of the document are called, this country had a legal system that enslaved African-Americans; and society deemed that women's work was primarily that of a wife, mother, and homemaker.

Eventually, after the Civil War, and many years of difficult struggle by women and men, the people of this country demanded that the Constitution be more just. Their efforts resulted in two very significant amendments to the Constitution. In 1865, slavery was forbidden with the enactment of the Thirteenth Amendment, which states:

> *Neither slavery nor involuntary servitude, except as a punishment for crime whereof the party shall have been duly convicted, shall exist within the United States, or any place subject to their jurisdiction.*

In 1920, women obtained the right to vote with the enactment of the Nineteenth Amendment, which states:

> *The rights of citizens of the United States to vote shall not be denied or abridged by the United States or by any State on account of sex.*

Both these amendments, as with all amendments to the Constitution, required approval by the Senate and the House of Representatives, and then two-thirds of the state legislatures. These requirements make it extremely difficult to change the Constitution. This is because its principles are considered so important that they should not be changed on a whim or just because one political party has gained substantial power.

2. A second source of rights are the laws created and enacted by the people we elect to Congress. These federal laws also apply to, and protect, all those living in this country from abuses of governmental power, and from abuses by private entities, such as corporations. An example of a federal law is

Title VII of the 1964 Civil Rights Act, which forbids discrimination by employers on the basis of one's race, gender, or national origin.

Sometimes Congress gives federal agencies, such as the Department of Labor, the task of enforcing its laws and may order the agencies to issue regulations that interpret those laws. The regulations, which are easier to create than actual laws, are intended to provide guidance to those who must enforce the law; they are especially useful for judges, who must apply the law itself to many different situations that Congress could not possibly have anticipated and addressed in the law itself.

3. A third source of rights are the laws created and enacted by the people we elect to state and city governments. Each state also has its own constitution. These laws apply only to those people living in that particular state or city. Sometimes they provide greater protection than federal laws or the federal Constitution. An example would be state laws that let victims of discrimination have more time in which to file a lawsuit than a federal law might allow.

4. A final source of law is called the common law. In our legal system, most legal concepts originally are developed in the decisions of judges. In deciding which legal doctrine applies to a particular case, each judge builds upon what other judges have done before. A judge's decision in a case is therefore said to constitute "precedent." Precedent means past decisions, and the body of legal doctrines created in this way is called the common law.

The common law is applicable in many situations, especially where laws are not specific enough to cover every situation. Judges will declare who is the winner of a lawsuit, and why, in a decision called an opinion. The opinions will then be considered by other judges when they deal with laws in other cases, and will be used by lawyers who seek to persuade a judge to find in her or his client's favor. If the facts involved in the prior decision are close to the facts in the present case, a judge will be strongly tempted to follow the former decision. He or she is not, however, required to do so except in the rare situation where the two cases are virtually identical. Even in this situation, if persuasive reasons are presented to show that the prior decision was wrong or ill-suited to changed conditions in society, the judge may not follow precedent.

Thus, while the Constitution provides a right to privacy, courts look to precedent to decide whether the right applies to everyone in all situations. For example, precedent has been very important in determining whether states can require minors to obtain parental consent prior to obtaining abortions. For example, let's say that a judge is presented with a lawsuit in which a teenager argues that her right to choose an abortion is threatened by a state law that requires her to first obtain the consent of both parents, one of whom may be opposed to abortion. The judge will (or should) read all prior decisions involving abortion in making a determination whether that particular law is constitutional.

Precedent makes it very difficult to get a judge to change, or overrule, a prior decision. Even controversial decisions, such as *Roe v. Wade*, which legalized the right to choose to have an abortion in this country, are not easily overruled. Thus, precedent plays a very influential role in whether someone can easily enforce her or his rights in any specific situation.

All of this means that it is generally not enough to know what a particular law says is illegal; you also have to know how judges have interpreted that law in specific situations. This is why it is important to have a lawyer. It is extremely difficult to determine how a law would apply to your situation if you are not familiar with the relevant common law.

What are criminal and civil laws?

Within the two major categories of law—federal and state—there are two subsets, criminal and civil laws. Criminal laws punish those who violate the law; they also impose penalties that can result in the loss of freedom. Possession of illegal drugs or guns, theft, and violent crimes—all are prosecuted under criminal laws, mostly under state laws in state court. All other laws are civil, and govern such areas as divorce, child custody, inheritance, fraud, contract enforcement, and discrimination.

How are laws created?

In the United States, laws are indirectly created by its citizens through the people that are elected to state and federal government. These elected officials have the power to make laws. This is why the right to vote is so important.

Each branch of government plays a role in the creation of laws. At the national level, the executive branch includes the office of the president, who through his or her signature turns a bill into a law; his or her top officials; and their governmental agencies. The judiciary includes all the federal courts, and is the place where laws are interpreted and enforced. The legislature (or Congress) includes the House of Representatives and the Senate, and is the place where laws are actually created. Each state has its own system based upon this model.

The creation of a law is a major process, requiring the approval by the three primary governmental entities: the House of Representatives, the Senate, and the president. Sometimes the idea for a particular law begins with one person, who is in a situation without legal protection. If many other people have had similar experiences, or also feel they have been unfairly treated, then they may contact their elected representatives (including their senators, mayors, representatives, and governors), gather signatures on petitions, write and send letters to those with influence and power, convene meetings designed to educate others about the problem, and gather support. An example might be state laws punishing drunk drivers, which were initiated by the relatives of people killed in car accidents.

Sometimes laws are created after a court makes a decision that many people feel is unfair, and that they want to change. One example is a federal law called the Civil Rights Restoration Act of 1991. Congress passed this law after a significant number of people in the country grew alarmed by several Supreme Court decisions that narrowed the protections created by Title VII, which prohibits discrimination in the workplace. The new law increases the protections of Title VII by, for example, allowing victims of discrimination to get more money from those found to have broken the law.

Finally, laws can be created when people gather enough signatures to put a proposed law on the ballot. This gives people an opportunity to vote for a law themselves, as opposed to letting their elected officials assume primary responsibility. Each state has its own requirements specifying the number of signatures that must be obtained, the time frame in which they must be gathered, and other important details.

What does a judge do?

Judges interpret federal and state laws. One group of judges are appointed to the federal courts by the president, where they primarily interpret federal laws and the federal Constitution. Another group of judges is either appointed by state governors, or are elected, to state courts, where they primarily interpret state laws and state constitutions.

Thus, there are two kinds of court systems: the federal court system and the state court system, although there are

7

substantial areas of overlap. For example, most crimes are prosecuted in state courts, although those crimes that allegedly violate federal laws are prosecuted in federal court. People go to state courts for family law disputes, such as divorce or child-custody proceedings. They must sue in federal court to enforce their rights under certain federal laws.

As you will see, judges have enormous power. If a judge believes that a federal or state laws contradicts the Constitution, she or he has the power to decide that the law is unconstitutional, and therefore that it is not a valid law. And if a judge believes that there is a conflict between a federal and state law, then he or she is required, by the Constitution, to enforce the federal law.

It is a judge's job to make sure that rights are enforced. A judge has the power to take many different kinds of action: she or he can impose a fine upon someone who broke a law, or put a criminal in jail, or make a decision about who gets custody of the children in the case of a divorce, or determine the amount of money that someone may be owed. People can go to jail or pay a fine if they disobey. Sometimes other authorities, such as federal and state administrative agencies or a labor arbitrator, can take remedial action. For example, many disputes between workers who belong to unions and their employers are dealt with by the National Labor Relations Board, which is a federal agency.

What is a case?

A case is the lawsuit started by a person, a group of people, or an entity (such as a corporation) against another. The plaintiff in a case is the person who sues. The defendant is the person or business or governmental agency that is sued. The legal writing in which the plaintiff states his or her grievance is called the complaint, which when filed in a court actually begins the lawsuit. Then the defendant files a response in the court called an answer. The legal writing that sets forth the law which applies, or that the plaintiffs or defendants believe should apply, is called the brief. Judges read the briefs from each side, and consider all of the arguments presented in making their decision.

One refers to a particular lawsuit by giving the names of the plaintiff or defendant. If Mary Jones sues Smith Corporation for allegedly refusing to hire her because she is a woman, her case will be called *Jones v. Smith Corporation.*

What if a plaintiff or defendant does not like a judge's decision?

If either side is unhappy with the results, they can take the case to the next higher-level court, and argue that the judge or jury applied the wrong legal concept to the facts. This is called an appeal, and the court in which the appeal is heard is called the appellate court. Both the federal and the state court systems have trial courts, which is where a case is first filed, then an intermediate appellate court, and then a court that is the highest, from which appeals may no longer be taken.

In the federal court system, the appellate courts are called circuit courts, and there are eleven circuits, each of which covers a specific geographical area in the country. The highest appellate court is the United States Supreme Court. In the state system, the highest state court is usually called the supreme court. The state courts operate independently from the federal court system. This means that they are administered separately and that the decisions made by judges in state courts do not affect federal law.

Not every appellate court will take an appeal from every trial court decision. In most cases, appellate courts have the right to refuse to reconsider a particular trial court's decision.

Moreover, appellate court judges do not usually reverse a trial court decision unless they believe that a significant error has been committed. This is because of an important principle that trial court judges are best equipped, since they hear all the evidence, to decide whose evidence is most persuasive.

Therefore, the odds that a trial court decision will be changed by an appellate court are not very great, and the chances become even smaller with every appeal. What happens during a trial, therefore, is extremely important, and having a good lawyer is absolutely essential.

Why is the Supreme Court so important?

The decisions of the Supreme Court have the most precedential value because there is no futher opportunity for appeal. The nine people who sit on the court, called justices, are appointed for life terms by the president. They cannot be fired or voted out of their jobs; they are thus insulated from public opinion, which may be hostile to their decisions, and that makes them very powerful.

All lower-court judges must abide by Supreme Court decisions unless a lawyer in a specific lawsuit can argue that a particular Supreme Court decision does not apply to the case at hand. When a lawyer does this it is called "distinguishing" the other case. A lawyer may distinguish a case because the people filing the case used another law or because the factual situation that gave rise to the court action is substantially different. An example would be a federal court decision stating that a wrongfully terminated employee cannot get extra damages unless he or she can show that the employer intended to harm him or her. A lawyer seeking to distinguish this case might let the court know that his or her client is suing under a state law that does not have such a requirement.

In rare cases, the Supreme Court may reverse itself. For

example, in 1873 the Supreme Court decided that the Constitution did not protect Myra Bradwell, who had graduated from law school but had not been allowed to practice law in Illinois. The reason stated by the justice writing the opinion: "The natural and proper timidity and delicacy which belongs to the female sex evidently unfits it for many occupations."[1] This decision prevented women from practicing law for many years, until, eventually, the Supreme Court decided that it had made the wrong decision.

Because justices are appointed for life terms, the chance to appoint a Supreme Court justice does not happen very often. The ability of the president to appoint a justice is one of her or his greatest powers; this makes it very important that we choose presidents who will appoint justices who will protect our rights and liberties. The same also applies to governors, who appoint judges to many of the state courts.

How can someone enforce a legal right?

Legal rights can be asserted in a number of different ways. Sometimes just mentioning that you are aware of your rights is enough to stop others from violating them. For example, merely raising a question of the legality of the actions of public officials will sometimes have a positive effect on those actions: public officials do not like to be accused of discrimination. And an indication of a readiness to file a lawsuit may convince officials that a person is serious about a claim for fair treatment, and they will take action to fix the problem.

Other times it is necessary to take further steps and actually file a lawsuit, which a young person cannot do alone. In most cases you must enlist the help of your relatives and an attorney, but you also can get special protection from the courts. If you already have a general guardian or other representative, that representative can sue on your behalf.

To start a lawsuit, you have to file a complaint in court. In both the federal and state court systems, you must start a lawsuit at the trial court level, where the facts are tried. This means that a jury or judge listens and watches as the lawyers present evidence of the facts that each side seeks to persuade the court are true and correct. Evidence can take many forms: for example, written documents, the testimony of a witness on the stand, photographs, and charts. Once a judge or jury has listened to and observed all the evidence presented by each side, they will choose the facts that they find believable, and decide which side has won.

It is important to keep in mind that lawsuits are expensive and can take a very long time, sometimes years. For low-income people, there are legal-aid or legal-services organizations who can help. You can find their phone numbers in your phone book, or contact your state American Civil Liberties Union. At the least, they may help you determine whether your rights have been violated.

Another alternative is to take group action. The first step in this process is education. Learn what your rights are. Read the Bill of Rights. Talk with your friends about what it means to have rights. If you think someone is discriminating against you, talk to your parents, other young men and women, teachers, and other knowledgeable people about possible solutions.

There are many ways you can protect yourself and others. Some possible ways are: write editorials to your school and local papers, form an organization, hold meetings, get elected to your student governing body, lobby school officials to change discriminatory policies, circulate petitions, work on the election campaigns of people you believe will protect your rights, organize a protest, speak to reporters.

It is important that you always be prepared by anticipating the potential objections to your arguments, and by developing thoughtful and appropriate responses that encourage discussion and resolution.

Are rights always fairly applied to all people?

No, although this is one of the great myths about law. Because there are so many different sources of rights, and because people from diverse backgrounds and beliefs enforce the laws, there is virtually no way to guarantee that laws are fairly applied. Nor do laws that set forth rights always do so with clarity or specificity. It is up to the courts, or administrative agencies, such as the Department of Labor, to interpret and flesh out the details; and in the process of doing so, many of the interpretations differ.

For example, two different courts may give completely different answers to the same question. This happens all the time in the federal appellate courts. One court may decide that workers wrongfully fired are entitled to more money than another court may allow. When this happens, the Supreme Court will eventually become involved and resolve the dispute. Thus, whether or not a person has a particular right may depend on which state or city he or she lives in.

The more times a particular issue is decided by a court, the more guidance there is in predicting what other judges or administrative personnel will decide. Similarly, the importance of the court or agency deciding a case, or the thoughtfulness of its reasoning, will help determine the effect of the decision. A judge whose decision is thorough, articulate, and well reasoned will have more influence than one whose decision is not.

Often, other factors that should not be relevant nonetheless wrongly affect the way that the law develops. Discrimination happens when people believe that certain personality traits, or physical abilities, are permanent and typical of all women (or all African-Americans, or all Hispanics, or all men, etc.). When

13

a person holds such a belief, such as that women are always better parents than men, then they are stereotyping. Stereotyping can lead to discrimination when laws or policies do not consider the individual woman, or Hispanic, or man, or senior citizen, for example, and her or his abilities. When laws or policies are created out of stereotypes, their application can never be fair or just.

Stereotyping women has taken many forms. In the early nineteenth century, many people relied upon certain verses in the Bible to justify their view that women were inferior. People referred to the story describing the birth of Eve from Adam's rib, for example, as proof of women's inferiority. Women were believed to be weak and irrational—victims of their bodily functions, especially menstruation, which was thought to affect their emotional state.

Stereotyping has frequently relied upon what is known as "bad science." We cannot automatically assume that all scientific developments are true or accurate simply because scientists are conducting experiments. Scientists themselves are real people, with their own prejudices, and these prejudices can influence the way they perform research, and the type of research that they choose to do.

For example, nineteenth-century scientists measured the size of women's skulls, the length of their bones, the rate of their breathing, and the number of their blood cells, all in order to prove that women were the weaker sex. In 1891 Dr. Henry M. Lyman wrote: "The mental activity necessary to prepare and recite her lessons demands the circulation of large quantities of blood through the brain. The girl has not blood enough to perform both lines of work at the same time. Menstruation slows her brain; study slows her menstruation."[2] These stereotypes were primarily used to keep white, upper-class women out of the workforce—not women of color or poor women, who were already working—and schools and to prevent them from voting.

The consequences were severe, affecting women in every sphere of life. Since women were perceived foremost to be at-home wives and mothers, scientists in the early decades of this century ignored the dangers confronting them from exposure to hazardous chemicals, among other things, in the workplace. And since scientists assumed that women's primary biological function was reproduction, health research for a long time focused mostly on men's health and diseases, except for problems related to reproduction.

While the worst overt discrimination no longer occurs, subtle barriers do remain today. For example, many studies report that people of color, such as African-Americans, receive longer prison sentences for their crimes than do white people. Other examples are discussed throughout this book.

Laws are also applied unfairly to the extent that rich people, who can afford to pay for the best lawyers and hire the best experts to gather the necessary evidence they need, often receive better treatment in the courts than do poor people.

2

SEX DISCRIMINATION

We hold these truths to be self-evident: that all men and women are created equal; that they are endowed by their Creator with certain inalienable rights; that among these are life, liberty, and the pursuit of happiness; that to secure these rights governments are instituted, deriving their just powers from the consent of the governed.

—from the Declaration of Sentiments and Resolutions

For many years women were not allowed to work in certain jobs and professions. They were not allowed to be lawyers, for example, and could be fired from their jobs if they became pregnant. The law was even harsher to a married woman. It deprived her of all rights, and made her husband her "master." It also gave her husband ownership of her property, including the wages she earned, full custody of their children in case of divorce, and the power to deprive her of liberty and to beat her. In several states, husbands were even protected from prosecution for raping their wives.

After years of difficult struggle, many of the worst laws were changed. One of the most important accomplishments was when women gained the right to vote with the ratification of the Nineteenth Amendment to the Constitution in 1920. (However, women of color for many years were unable to completely exercise that right. This is because states and cities often engaged in practices, such as literacy tests, that were designed to make it difficult for people to vote. Other factors have discouraged people from voting, such as geographic proximity to voting places.) Eventually, women won other rights too, including more control over their property and wages as well as the right to custody of their children in divorce.

While many of the most unjust and inhumane laws disappeared, not all gender-based laws were abolished by the middle of the twentieth century. As late as the 1970s, there continued to be laws that prevented women from working extra hours to earn overtime pay when a man could; that allowed men to have sole control over property owned jointly with their wives; that denied fringe benefits to working women when working men got those benefits automatically; and that allowed young women to obtain financial support from parents only until they turned eighteen while young men could receive such assistance until the age of twenty-one. Government officials could and did decide that female high-school students had to take homemaking and could not play competitive sports, like football, and that a low-income woman who wanted to enter a government-training program had to wait until all low-income men had the chance to do so.

As these examples illustrate, sex discrimination can be overt—as when women get fired from a job because they are pregnant—and it can be subtle, as is often the case when women are sexually harassed on the job. And it does not always happen because someone *intends* to discriminate. It can happen even where the *consequences* of an action or policy are discriminatory.

One example of a practice that resulted in a discriminatory *effect* during the 1980s was when New York State used the Standardized Aptitude Test (SAT) to determine who would get college scholarships. While no one intended for girls to get fewer scholarships than boys in 1989, several high-school girls, with the help of the American Civil Liberties Union, were able to convince a judge, in a case called *Sharif v. New York State Department of Education*, that the use of the SAT, which is intended to predict college performance in the first year, should not be used to determine scholarship awards. The judge looked at evidence showing that although 53 percent of applicants for state merit scholarships in 1986 and 1987 were girls, they received only 43 percent of the scholarships and concluded that this discrepancy meant that use of the test had an unlawful and discriminatory effect against girls.[1]

WHAT IS SEX DISCRIMINATION?

Does sex discrimination still happen today?

Yes. Women represent a large and ever-growing percentage of the workforce that remains confined to low-paying, low-status jobs with little or no opportunity for advancement. Women suffer sexual harassment in the workplace. Women who work outside the home still are expected by society to be primarily responsible for the care of the home, children, and elderly family members, while men are not.

The fight against sex discrimination continues for young women as well. They are fighting for the right to an educational environment free of harassment, and for the right to custody of their children. Many are fighting for the right to choose to have an abortion, what they call the right to control their own bodies. What follows are stories of several young women who have recently had to seek legal help to stop discrimination.

Christine Franklin and Shannon Faulkner: Discrimination in Education

For many girls, their ability to learn in a safe and supportive environment is hindered by sexual harassment by teachers or other students. In one recent case, Georgia high-school student Christine Franklin told a court that "beginning in the fall of 1986 . . . I was in the tenth grade, [and] was subjected to a continuing course of intentional sexual harassment, culminating in forced intercourse, by Andrew Hill, a sports coach and teacher employed by the District."[2] School officials initially ignored her complaints. It was not until March 1988 that they launched an official investigation. Once they did, the investigator quickly concluded that the sexual-harassment allegations were true, and school officials forced the teacher to resign.

In the meantime, Ms. Franklin filed a complaint with the Department of Education, which enforces the law that prohibits sex discrimination in schools receiving federal funds. The department concluded that Hill's resignation, and the school's implementation of grievance procedures (the way in which a complaint is filed, who listens to both sides, the rules that are followed, etc.) were enough to solve the problem. But Ms. Franklin did not agree. She brought a lawsuit to recover money damages as well, and took her case, *Franklin v. Gwinnett County School District*,[3] all the way to the Supreme Court and won.

Discrimination in admissions to certain schools is another problem, especially where there continues to exist stereotypes about the ability of girls to be sufficiently aggressive. For example, high-school senior Shannon Faulkner sought admittance to the Citadel, an all-male military college in South Carolina. The Citadel addressed its provisional acceptance to "Mr. Shannon Richey Faulkner." As soon as the school realized that Faulkner was female, however, it rescinded that acceptance.

In a long legal battle, Ms. Faulkner won the right to attend the school in the case *Faulkner v. Jones*.[4] She entered the freshman program in the fall of 1995 as the school's only female cadet. Unfortunately, she left after one week, explaining that the stress of the lawsuit had finally caught up with her. However, demonstrating the positive impact one person can have, the next year the Citadel admitted four women. Two have withdrawn from the program, which indicates that it may take some time for the Citadel environment to adequately welcome women and make possible their success.

Jane Hodgson: Discrimination in Abortion

In 1989, several Minnesota teenagers took a case to the Supreme Court. Each of the six young women had become pregnant and made the personal and difficult decision to obtain an abortion. At the time, however, a Minnesota law forbade abortions—in most cases, on women under eighteen years of age—until at least 48 hours after both of her parents had been notified. Two doctors and four medical clinics joined the six women in challenging that restriction, saying that it limited a woman's right to control what happens to her body.

The case, called *Hodgson v. Minnesota*,[5] ended when the Supreme Court decided that the requirement that both parents be notified before a minor could obtain an abortion violated the Constitution because it placed too great a burden on young women. The Court went on to say, however, that the requirement was legal when coupled with a judicial bypass procedure, which allows young women to get around notifying their parents by going to court and convincing a judge that they are mature enough to make their own decision. So, while the teens won a partial victory in court, certain restrictions still remain.

Jennifer Ireland: Discrimination against Single Mothers

Young women may be discriminated against when they do not fulfill the traditional expectations that women should stay at home with their children. For example, when in Michigan fifteen-year-old Jennifer Ireland became pregnant, she chose to keep her baby girl, Maranda. Steve Smith, Maranda's father, had no contact with Maranda until she was one year old, when he began visiting her. While Ms. Ireland finished high school, her mother helped care for Maranda. When Ms. Ireland received a scholarship to the University of Michigan, she took Maranda to live in university housing and put her daughter in day care while she attended classes.

But when Ms. Ireland filed for child support, Mr. Smith, who was attending a community college, filed for permanent custody of Maranda, charging Ms. Ireland with child neglect. At trial, the judge weighed several factors in determining what was in the best interests of the child. Despite Ms. Ireland's accusations that Mr. Smith had been physically abusive during their relationship, the court ruled that both sides had valid cases, but the determining factor in his decision had to do with day care.

The judge stated, "The mother's academic pursuits, although laudable, are demanding and in order to complete her program it necessitates the leaving of the child for a consider-able portion of its life in the care of strangers."[6] The judge thus ruled that Maranda would be better off with Mr. Smith, whose mother is a full-time homemaker and could care for Maranda while Mr. Smith attended school.

This decision was ultimately reversed by an appellate court, which sent the case back to the trial court but to a different judge. That judge awarded joint custody to both parents. Ms. Ireland has since dropped out of college and moved back into her mother's home so that she can be closer to Mr. Smith's residence to make the sharing of custody easier.

Jacqueline Lantz: Discrimination in Sports

In 1985, sixteen-year-old Jacqueline Lantz, who wanted to try out for her junior varsity football team in Yonkers, New York, got a better reception from the courts when she challenged a New York rule that stated: "There shall be no mixed competition in the following sports: basketball, boxing, football, ice hockey, rugby and wrestling."[7] The commissioner of the New York State Department of Education tried to show that, as a general rule, female high-school students are weaker than their male counterparts, and thus the rule was necessary to protect their health and safety. The commissioner asserted, "It makes no difference that there might be a few girls who wish to play football who are more physically fit than some of the boys on the team."[8]

The judge in the case rejected that reasoning as discriminatory, stating that the effect of the regulation is to exclude qualified members of one gender because they are presumed to suffer from an inherent handicap or to be innately inferior.[9] Thus, he declared that the rule was illegal because it violated the Constitution (the equal-protection clause of the Fourteenth Amendment), and ordered Ms. Lantz to be allowed to try out for the team. Not only did she make the squad, but her legal victory paved the way for another young woman to become a running back at a nearby high school that same season.

What has caused the laws relating to discrimination to change?

Much hard work by many women and men. One of the first major efforts occurred almost 150 years ago, in 1848, when hundreds of women met in Seneca Falls, New York, at a convention organized by prominent women's rights activists Elizabeth Cady Stanton and Lucretia Mott. They, and all the other women at the convention, outlined the "unjust laws" they were protesting, in a famous document called the Declaration of Sentiments, which is reproduced in the Appendix. The declaration commented that when the law deprived women of the right to vote, it deprived them of "this first right of a citizen."

However, eliminating slavery was an essential prerequisite before *all* women in this country could obtain the rights until then reserved for men. Until slavery was abolished, many, such as the famous antislavery advocate Frederick Douglass, would not work for the rights of women in general, believing that any rights obtained would benefit only white women, and that black people needed electoral power (the right to vote) even more.

Real equality for women of color has remained an elusive dream as more subtle barriers to their equal participation in society have remained. One example is in the voting arena, as discussed earlier. Another area has been in the provision of Social Security and Supplementary Security Income benefits. In 1992, the *New York Times* reported that the Social Security Administration had found evidence of discrimination against African-American applicants: the study found that white applicants for disability insurance benefits had an 8 percent better chance of receiving benefits after being turned down, while those who applied for supplementary security income had a

4 percent advantage over black applicants.[10] Eliminating those barriers, which still exist today in some places, continues to be an essential priority in the struggle for equality.

A more recent effort in which the struggle for equality took place was the fight for the Equal Rights Amendment (ERA) during the 1970s. Because of the many discriminatory laws and practices—and because at that time there appeared to be little chance that courts would invalidate them—activists sought to amend the Constitution to guarantee that "Equality of rights under the law shall not be denied or abridged by the United States or by any State on account of sex."

The amendment, although first proposed in 1923, only gained political momentum with the rebirth of the feminist movement in the 1970s, and was finally approved by Congress in 1972. But its supporters were unable to get the required 38, or two-thirds, of the states to ratify. On June 30, 1982, the ERA was officially declared dead.

Feminists, of course, decried this loss. But the demise of the ERA masked a larger victory. In the same decade in which the ERA was defeated, women and men transformed sex-discrimination law in this country. This was due partly to economic necessity; as more families needed to have two wage earners, more women entered the workforce. This put pressure on employers to treat women fairly and led to the dissolution of many stereotypes and the creation of many good laws.

Additionally, many people learned to challenge the stereotypes that had been causing them to limit their goals and to recognize their needs even if they ran against stereotypes. Thus, many women recognized that they really did not want to work at home. Many men grew to understand the need for housekeeping chores to be shared.

Eventually, changing ideas about the roles of women and men influenced the Supreme Court and caused the justices to declare some laws to be invalid that had earlier been approved by previous justices. For example, the Supreme Court made a number of significant decisions that determined that specific state laws were illegal, including a Louisiana law that made the husband the "head and master" with sole control over property jointly owned with his wife,[11] a Missouri law that gave working husbands, but only some working wives, death benefits for their surviving spouses,[12] and a Utah law that required parents to give child support to young women to the age of eighteen but to young men to the age of twenty-one.[13]

Feminist pressure produced results in other areas as well. Congress and state legislatures rewrote old laws to eliminate sex-discriminatory provisions and passed new laws to outlaw gender discrimination in such diverse areas as employment, education, credit, and housing. And federal and state agencies began taking more seriously the enforcement of laws prohibiting discrimination on the job.

What is the women's rights movement?

While people sometimes refer to a "women's rights movement" when they want to talk about the collective efforts to combat gender discrimination, it really is not accurate to say that there is a *single* women's rights movement. The movement, both historically and at the present time, consists of many diverse groups of women: women of different economic status, women from different racial and ethnic groups, women with disabilities, lesbians, and elderly women, among others. Men have participated as well.

Many of these groups have formed local and national organizations to focus intensively on their own priority issues. For example, these organizations include the National Black Women's Health Project (Atlanta, Georgia), the National Latina Health Organization (Oakland, California), the Native American Health Education Resource Center (Lake Andes, South Dakota), and the National Women of Color Reproductive Health Coalition (Washington, D.C.). This diversity of individuals and organizations has generated tensions and conflicting approaches about how to solve the same problems, although the general environment has been one where many values and goals are held in common.

For instance, many believe that all laws that treat women and men differently should be illegal. Those taking this approach (equality) have argued that singling out women for special treatment reinforces the stereotype that women are more able parents than men, and that it discourages men from assuming responsibility for parenting. They feel it makes women less desirable employees and thus encourages discrimination.

Others believe that there are some differences between women and men that justify special treatment. Since only women can become pregnant, those in this group believe that there should be special laws that provide benefits to women concerning pregnancy-related issues, such as maternity leave. Proponents of special treatment claim that to ignore biology-based differences ignores the extra burden that pregnancy and child care place on women. This has been a difficult debate within the women's movement, and it is far from settled.

A sophisticated network of organizations, which direct their work to addressing specific issues and needs, makes it easier to respond to discrimination problems that persist today. The examples of Christine Franklin, Jacqueline Lantz, Shannon Faulkner, Jane Hodgson, and Jennifer Ireland demonstrate how important it remains for people to work together to change society, including its laws. They also indicate how important it is for women to increase their representation on the nation's courts and legislative bodies. Until those numbers improve, women simply cannot be assured that laws will truly reflect their needs. Once that goal is achieved, women will be closer to the goal of equality, although *real* equality will not be achieved until all stereotypes are eliminated from both men's *and* women's beliefs.

WHAT LEGAL RIGHTS DO WOMEN HAVE?

As discussed in the first chapter of this book, there are two fundamental sources of laws in this country. In the federal sphere, there is the Constitution and the laws created by Congress. These laws affect all people living in the United States. In the state sphere, there are state constitutions and the laws created by state legislatures and city governments. These laws affect those people living in a particular state or city. This section will describe some of the most important laws that affect your rights.

How does the federal Constitution protect women's rights?

Probably the most important part of the Constitution that protects women is called the equal-protection clause of the Fourteenth Amendment. It states: "No state shall . . . deny to any person within its jurisdiction the equal protection of the laws."

This clause forbids states from treating its citizens in different ways. Historically, this law has been used to combat discrimination directed against African-Americans: segregated public schools, denial of voting rights, and segregation in public areas, such as restaurants. But the concept of equal protection has also been used to protect the rights of other groups, such as immigrants, ethnic minorities, and women. State legislatures and Congress must create laws that apply equally to

African-Americans and whites, to Hispanics and Anglos, and that do not single out one group for favored treatment over another. Thus, for example, if a state legislature passes a law favoring one group, using race as a classification, judges will (or should) declare that law unconstitutional.

However, not all attempts to classify people violate the Constitution. In fact, most do not. In a variety of contexts, state laws can and do single out different classes of citizens for different treatment. For example, people over the age of sixteen who have passed a state driver's test may drive; people under age sixteen (depending on state law) and those who have not passed the test may not drive. Such distinctions are valid under the equal-protection clause. It is only when a classification is based upon stereotypes primarily about race or gender that it will be declared invalid.

Does the federal Constitution protect everyone?

No. The Constitution forbids only federal, state, and local governments and agencies to discriminate, not private companies or individuals. This prohibition covers a broad range of governmental activities—from passing discriminatory laws to engaging in discriminatory practices—but is still limited to action in which the government is involved. Thus, a public-school official may not bar women from a physics class. But it would not violate the Constitution if a private-school official made the same decision.

How can someone prove to a judge that there has been unlawful gender discrimination in violation of the federal Constitution?

It is fairly difficult. In 1976, the Supreme Court decided that it would ask two questions after finding that sex discrimination exists: *Does the law further an important goal of the govern-*

ment? And is the different treatment of men and women closely related to the achievement of that goal? If the answer to either of these questions is no, the law is unconstitutional. Each of these questions is called a test.

The Supreme Court first applied this test in *Craig v. Boren*,[14] a case filed by a young attorney, Ruth Bader Ginsburg, then director of the American Civil Liberties Union's Women's Rights Project, who went on to become a justice on the Supreme Court. She represented a young man who believed that an Oklahoma law that forbade the sale of beer to men under twenty-one years old, but prohibited sale only to women under eighteen, violated the Constitution. The young man claimed that this law unfairly assumed that girls over eighteen years old can better handle alcohol than boys the same age.

The state of Oklahoma defended the law by arguing that it would improve traffic safety—a worthy state objective. However, after examining Oklahoma's statistics on driving while intoxicated, the Supreme Court concluded that the statistical differences in the behavior of young men and women were too insignificant to justify denying the sale of beer to young men of the same age group.

Thus, although driving safely might be an important goal, the Supreme Court decided that treating men and women differently in this situation was not closely related to the accomplishment of that goal. The Court reasoned that other efforts, such as improved education about the dangers of drinking and driving, and better enforcement of drunk-driving laws, would have a more direct and better effect on traffic safety.

The test used in sex-discrimination cases is not as rigorous as that used in cases of race discrimination. This has become even more true in recent years as conservative judges who believe in specific roles for women and men have increasingly been appointed to the federal courts.[15]

The federal Constitution does not bar all sex-based distinctions in the law, but only those that fail this test.

Are there any acts of discrimination that are not protected under the federal Constitution?

Yes. The Supreme Court has refused to apply these same constitutional protections to pregnant women. Also, the Supreme Court has refused to view abortion cases as affecting women's right to equality, and has looked at these cases only as affecting women's right to privacy. This difference is important, and is discussed in chapter 4. The Supreme Court also has refused to apply the protections of the Constitution to cases in which the government claims a national-security interest, such as where women have challenged the all-male draft registration.[16]

Are there any other federal constitutional rights that protect women from discrimination?

Yes. Many women have asserted that the right to privacy, which courts have found exists implicitly (although not mentioned explicitly) in several provisions of the Constitution, protects their right to practice birth control and to choose abortion.

But this chapter has focused mainly on the concept of equal treatment because women have cited that protection most frequently to challenge gender-discrimination practices.

Does the Constitution protect women from being stereotyped and from other subtle barriers to equality?

No. The Constitution, as interpreted by the Supreme Court, addresses itself only to overt acts of intentional discrimination.[17] It does not deal with the subtle and complex barriers to women's equality, such as stereotyping, the lack of decent and affordable child care, and programs to care for the elderly and the ill. These are burdens that fall disproportionately on women. However, they can still be addressed through legislative and other political action. For example, laws that require state governments to set up effective mechanisms to collect child support from fathers help keep women and their children out of poverty.

Do states have equal-rights laws?

As you may remember from chapter 1, all states have their own constitutions. Many of these state constitutions contain special provisions to prohibit gender discrimination, such as equal rights amendments (ERAs) that typically say something like: *No person shall discriminate on the basis of sex*. Such a provision is another powerful tool for fighting sex discrimination because state courts can decide that their own constitutions provide more protection than the federal Constitution.

A state ERA may protect against both governmental and private discrimination. (Remember that the federal Constitution does not protect people against discrimination by private individuals or businesses.) In addition, many state courts use a stricter test in gender-discrimination cases brought under the state's ERA than the federal courts are willing to use in equal-protection cases. This makes it easier to challenge discrimination in those states.

Sixteen states—Alaska, Colorado, Connecticut, Hawaii, Illinois, Maryland, Massachusetts, Montana, New Hampshire, New Mexico, Pennsylvania, Texas, Utah, Virginia, Washington, and Wyoming—have ERAs. Also, New Jersey in effect adopted an ERA in 1947 when it amended the equal-protection provision in its constitution to apply to "persons" instead of "men." Similarly, judges in California currently interpret the equal-protection clause in its constitution to prohibit most forms of sex discrimination.

The largest number of sex-discrimination cases has arisen

31

in the area of family law. State ERAs have been used to invalidate different age minimums for marriage for men and women; allow men and women to claim the same reasons for needing a divorce; expand the obligation for spousal support at divorce; and invalidate common-law presumptions that household goods acquired during marriage belong to the husband. State ERAs have also been used to improve educational opportunities for girls, both in the classroom and in athletic programs. For example, advocates used the Pennsylvania ERA to successfully challenge the men-only admissions policy of a city high school. High-school girls also used the Pennsylvania ERA to challenge their exclusion from the Pennsylvania Interscholastic Athletic Association;[18] in the 30 years since this ruling, there has been a significant increase in the number of women participating in basketball, soccer, track and field, gymnastics, softball, field hockey, and lacrosse.

Women have also used state ERAs to attack economic discrimination. For example, in Pennsylvania, women used the state ERA to eliminate gender differences in insurance rates. And in Colorado, women used their state ERA to challenge a health-insurance policy that would not cover medical expenses associated with pregnancy.

Are there other laws that prohibit sex discrimination?

Yes. Several federal, state, and city laws also prohibit gender discrimination. There are four major federal laws that forbid discrimination against women workers by private and public employers.

Title VII of the 1964 Civil Rights Act prohibits discrimination in employment, and specifically pregnancy discrimination. It applies to employers, unions, and employment agencies. It reaches most cases of discrimination and holds out the best hope of an effective remedy.

The **Equal Pay Act** forbids companies from paying women who are doing the same work as men less than they pay those men. A woman who believes she has been discriminated against may bring a lawsuit, or file a grievance with the Equal Employment Opportunity Commission.

Executive Orders 11246 and 11375, issued by President Johnson in 1965 and 1967, require any employer that has a contract with the federal government not to discriminate.[19] The agency that enforces these orders is oriented more toward setting up affirmative-action plans than toward compensating women for past discrimination.

The **Age Discrimination Act of 1967** prohibits discrimination against workers who are a minimum of 40 years old.[20] This law is important because many women who have stayed at home raising children try to enter the job market when they are older and may face age discrimination.

Each of these laws is discussed in more detail in chapter 6.

Are the rights of women under age eighteen different from those women eighteen and over?

Yes. The most obvious difference lies in the age requirements for driving a car, voting in elections, and drinking alcohol. There are also age requirements for getting married, entering into contracts, and writing wills. In some cities, minors have a curfew in the evening, where after a certain hour they cannot be on the streets unless accompanied by an adult.

3

YOUR MIND

"Those who trust us, educate us."

—George Eliot

Your greatest resource is your mind. But it needs constant attention, stimulation, and discipline to be at its best. To grow beautiful flowers, a person needs first to make sure that the garden soil is properly fed and that there is adequate sun. Your school is like the soil; if it has good teachers, challenging courses, and a variety of extracurricular activities, and if everyone, boys and girls, can all equally take advantage of what is offered, then it will help create strong, healthy minds.

But it takes attentive gardeners to make sure that the soil is rich in nutrients. In the U.S. educational system, many have had to fight vigorously to ensure that all students equally receive its benefits. It may be hard to believe, but there was a time in this country when women were not allowed to attend college, and when girls were discouraged from attending school because it was assumed that they would simply become wives and mothers and that their education was therefore not important.

In 1836, Oberlin College became the first college to admit women. Even so, for a long time Oberlin women were not allowed to take the same courses as men, because it was thought that their minds were not of the same quality as men's. Some women were required to take care of men by washing their clothes, cleaning their rooms, and serving their meals. Some were not even allowed to speak at school functions. Lucy Stone, an early Oberlin graduate, refused to write a commencement essay because a male student would have read it to the audience.[1]

By invoking the federal Constitution, women and girls have successfully sued public elementary, junior high, and senior high schools, as well as state colleges and universities, to combat gender discrimination. Women scored an important victory in 1970, for example, when they gained admission to the previously all-male University of Virginia at Charlottesville, the most prestigious school of the state's university system.[2] High-school students knocked down all-male barriers at the highly rated Stuyvesant High School in New York City and at the prestigious Boston Latin school in Massachusetts.

In the 1970s, Congress passed a variety of laws to combat other forms of sex discrimination in education. For instance, Congress passed Title IX of the Education Amendments of 1972 Act,[3] a federal law that forbids gender discrimination in public and private schools—from preschool through graduate level—that receive federal money. It even applies to religious schools, although specific practices may be exempt (for instance, segregated physical-education classes).

Congress has passed other laws too, each of which applies either to specific situations, or specific types of education. For example, the Public Health Services Act protects students in the health professions;[4] Title II of the 1976 Amendments to the Vocational Education Act of 1963 protects students in vocational schools;[5] Title IV of the 1964 Civil Rights Act allows attorney generals—the chief lawyer who works for each state—to sue public schools and colleges for sex-discriminatory policies.[6] And the Equal Educational Opportunities Act of 1974 declares that "all children enrolled in public schools are entitled to equal educational opportunity without regard to race, color, sex or national origin."[7]

These laws, however, and the agency regulations that interpret them, have not provided complete protection against discrimination. Each law has its weaknesses. For example, the Equal Educational Opportunities Act does not mention segregation by sex or employment discrimination. Evidence that discrimination still exists is reflected in the small number of women in top administrative and faculty positions, the exclusion of women from many sports, and the severe underfunding and lack of support for women's sports in general. These problems are exacerbated by the tendency of standardized tests—when used alone (without looking, for example, at school grades and other measures of performance) to determine admissions, placements, and the allocation of scholarships—to discriminate against women.

Can girls attend all-male schools?

Under the federal Constitution, the answer has sometimes been yes and sometimes no. In an important 1982 case brought by the American Civil Liberties Union, the Supreme Court ruled that men could not be excluded from the School of Nursing at the Mississippi University for Women.[8] Justice O'Connor, the first woman to sit on the Supreme Court, wrote the opinion and stated that the all-women policy reinforced traditional stereotypes of nursing as a woman's profession.

In another case, a group of young women achieved an important victory in 1984 when they used their state equal rights amendment to obtain admission to the previously all-male Central High, one of Philadelphia's two public high schools whose focus is to prepare all its students for college.[9]

And most recently, a district court in Michigan ruled that the opening of an all-male public school by the Detroit board of education could be blocked as illegally denying women the right to equal educational opportunities.[10] The board justified the all-male school by saying that the academy was experimental and the data collected from the three-year project would also benefit female students. Although the board argued that coeducational programs had not adequately met the needs of young urban men, the court decided that school officials had presented "no evidence that the educational system is failing urban males because females attend school with males."

Still unanswered is whether public schools that are segregated, but offer substantially the same quality of education, also violate the Constitution.

Title IX, the federal law that prohibits discrimination by all educational institutions that receive federal money, also prohibits one-sex schools. However, it affects only undergraduate, graduate, professional, and vocational schools that accept federal money. If a school does not take that money, then it can exclude either sex.

In addition, regulations created by the Department of Health, Education and Welfare, which interpret Title IX, allow school officials to discriminate in admissions for preschool, elementary and secondary schools (both public and private); private undergraduate colleges; public undergraduate colleges that have always been single-sex institutions; and military schools.

Such schools can exclude women completely, set up a quota system to limit their enrollment, or even demand that women meet higher admissions standards than men. A woman denied admission to one of these schools could still sue under the federal Constitution, and in the process attack the Title IX provision as unconstitutional. In fact, this is what Joe Hogan did in his successful effort to attend the Mississippi University for Women.

As you can see, not all laws apply equally to all schools. This makes it difficult to figure out whether a particular practice at a particular school is illegal.

Are single-sex schools better for girls?

Some believe that girls benefit from single-sex schools. They point to studies that show that women who have graduated from single-sex colleges in previous decades have moved into a high number of leadership roles in later life.[11]

However, at the time those women attended single-sex colleges, many of the country's most prestigious colleges—including Harvard, Yale, and Princeton as well as many smaller, high-quality colleges and the military academies—did not admit women at all. Thus, the most talented women of previous generations who desired to attend highly selective institutions often had little choice but to attend all-women's colleges. These studies have not been repeated because the barriers to women in the once all-male schools have been largely eliminated.

One problem with all-male schools is that they perpetuate the idea that women cannot compete with men in an academic setting, which is simply not the case. Nowadays, the vast majority of talented young women are "voting with their feet" by not applying to single-sex colleges in sufficient numbers to keep them viable.

Do girls have the right to take the same courses as boys and to refuse to take girls-only courses?

Yes, with a few exceptions. The Title IX regulations do not allow a girl (or boy) to be excluded from a class or activity because of gender; they also don't allow separate courses to be offered to boys or girls. A few girls have succeeded in challenging discriminatory course assignments—such as metalworking for boys and home economics for girls—under the equal-protection clause.[12] And some states, such as New York and Massachusetts, have laws that specifically forbid the exclusion of either sex from courses.

These laws apply to courses in health, physical education, industrial arts, business, vocational and technical subjects, home economics, and music. Schools may group students in physical education according to physical ability and may separate girls and boys for participation in wrestling, boxing, rugby, ice hockey, football, basketball, and other contact sports. However, several state courts have allowed girls to compete on boys' teams even if there are separate girls' teams and even if they are contact sports.

Sex-education classes may also be held in separate sessions for girls and boys in elementary and secondary schools but not in post-secondary education.[13] Choruses that are selected on the basis of vocal range are permitted to be one—or predominantly one—sex.

May school counselors steer girls into courses "suitable" for females or advise them to prepare for jobs that women have traditionally held?

No. Yet this is still common because it is a hard practice to stop. Counselors, sometimes unaware of their own biases, indirectly promote male-only courses, like woodworking, by channeling girls into more "feminine" fields, or discourage girls from taking what may be considered masculine subjects like physics or calculus.[14]

Schools that discover that a disproportionate number of boys or girls are enrolled in a particular course or program of study are required to investigate the school's counseling or testing program, but it is doubtful that such self-monitoring is very effective.

One potential area of trouble lies with some of the standardized vocational-interest tests that many counselors use to help people make the "right" career choice. Counselors have used different questionnaires for boys and girls or evaluated boys' and girls' answers according to different standards so that a boy and a girl giving the same answers received different career advice. For example, they may rate a boy's aptitude for jobs traditionally held by men, and a girl's for jobs traditionally held by women, rather than rating both boys and girls for all jobs. Such discriminatory tests and counseling materials are now forbidden for school use.

May schools use textbooks that show women in traditionally female jobs or that contain other sexual stereotypes?

Yes. Although gender-based textbooks tend to subtly encourage girls into adopting subservient "female" roles and reinforce the stereotypes of women as passive, dependent, over emotional creatures, the regulations issued under Title IX specifically exempt textbooks and other curricular materials from coverage under the law. The reason is a possible conflict with the First Amendment to the Constitution, which protects freedom of speech and press from governmental interference.

However, there may be other avenues to address this issue. For example, California law requires schools to use instructional materials that portray the contributions of women in all fields; it also forbids the use of materials that treat women as inferior.[15] Many women's groups work to develop unbiased textbooks, educational materials, and courses to eliminate sex-role stereotyping.[16]

May schools exclude pregnant students or unwed mothers?

No, although pregnancy is the main reason that girls leave school. Title IX regulations forbid schools to exclude pregnant students or students who have had a child or an abortion.[17] Pregnant students may ask to attend special schools or educational programs, but their requests must be truly voluntary.

Schools are not allowed to pressure pregnant students into withdrawing from regular courses, or refuse to allow them to return after their babies are born. A pregnant student must also be allowed to take a leave of absence for as long as her doctor thinks necessary and later resume attendance, even though her school might not allow leaves of absence. If a school maintains a separate, voluntary program for pregnant girls, it must be comparable in quality to that offered other students.

In addition to laws prohibiting discrimination on the basis of pregnancy, a number of states—including California, the District of Columbia, Florida, Minnesota, New York, Oregon, Rhode Island, and Wisconsin—also have laws or programs designed to encourage pregnant and parenting students to remain in school and to provide various services to these students.

May schools prohibit the enrollment of married students?

No. Courts recognize that married students need an education as much as single students, although early laws did bar married students. Now Title IX regulations forbid school officials from even asking about a student's marital status.

May students who are pregnant, married, or parents be excluded from extracurricular activities?

No. Judges have supported married girls' and boys' efforts to participate in chess and drama clubs, choir, varsity sports, and other activities, because these activities are an essential part of education, and because exclusion from such activities violates young people's fundamental right to marry.[18]

At least one recent decision, however, suggests that the National Honor Society, which admits students on the basis of character, leadership, service, and scholarship, can exclude pregnant girls on the grounds of "immorality."[19]

May girls be excluded from college fraternities and other organizations?

Yes, college sororities and fraternities may limit membership to one gender. Also, the YMCA, YWCA, Girl Scouts, Boy Scouts, and Camp Fire Girls may exclude members of the opposite sex. Schools can sponsor mother-daughter and father-son events, but if such activities are provided for boys, girls must be given the opportunity for reasonably comparable activities.[20]

Can colleges segregate men and women in living facilities?

Title IX specifically allows living facilities to be segregated by sex. Schools that provide housing for men must also provide housing for women that is comparable in quality and cost. For instance, a university cannot house its male students in two-room private suites while crowding its female students into dormitory doubles. In addition, schools must take steps to ensure that off-campus housing is available to men and women on the same terms. Also, colleges may not apply different housing rules and regulations to women and men, charge them different fees, or offer different benefits or services, such as free cleaning for men only. Campus residency requirements, curfews, and other such rules for women, which were once common, are now also illegal.

May educational institutions award scholarships that are restricted to one sex or discriminate in the award of financial aid?

The Title IX regulations forbid gender discrimination in financial assistance. Schools may not give students different types or amounts of financial aid based on gender, nor may they use different eligibility requirements for males and females. For instance, a school may not give scholarships to all men with a 3.0 average but only to women who have a 3.5 average. Nor may a school award larger scholarships to men than to women with the same financial need.

However, Title IX regulations allow schools to administer gender-restricted scholarships and fellowships established by will or trust or by foreign governments (the Rhodes Scholarships, for example, were once restricted to men) so long as the overall effect is not to discriminate against women. This is determined by looking at the overall distribution of scholarships by gender.

Are women protected against sexual harassment in schools?

Yes. Title IX prohibits sexual harassment, as illustrated by the case involving Christine Franklin, discussed in chapter 2. Teachers can also sue under Title VII of the 1964 Civil Rights Act, which prohibits discrimination by certain employers. The only difference between Title IX and Title VII is that Title VII has a ceiling on the amount of money that a victim can recover.

43

Can girls participate in all school athletic programs?

Sometimes yes, sometimes no. It depends mostly on where you live. The regulations mandate "equal athletic opportunities" for both sexes, although they do not require equal amounts of money to be spent on boys and girls. Still, some girls have improved inadequate girls' sports programs by filing lawsuits challenging different spending for girls' and boys' programs— lawsuits that led the schools to spend more on girls' programs.[21]

The reason that some girls have fought for integrated athletic programs is that they provide the opportunity for the most athletically talented girls to compete with athletically talented boys. Funding of nontraditional sports, like golf, cross-country skiing, tennis, and soccer, and equal funding of sports for both boys and girls, has led to more opportunities for girls not interested in traditional male sports like football to find a sport of interest. This also benefits those boys who are not interested in or lack the athletic ability for sports like football. Eventually, schools might find themselves providing meaningful athletic programs for all students, allowing individuals to choose sports by interest and skill rather than by their gender.

For many years, girls were forced to sue their schools, citing the Constitution or state antidiscrimination laws, to challenge their exclusion from all-male teams. And they have largely succeeded, especially in noncontact sports.[22] These challenges were most effective when schools were without girls' teams at all.

4

YOUR BODY

*Parents can only give good advice or put them on the right path, but
the final forming of a person's character lies in their own hands.*

—Anne Frank, *Diary*

This chapter focuses on the right that is sometimes called the
right to "reproductive freedom." Reproductive freedom means
that a woman's or girl's privacy is protected when she seeks
medical advice and treatment for birth control, sexually transmitted diseases, pregnancy tests, prenatal care, childbirth, and
abortions. It means having convenient and affordable access to
reproductive health care, contraceptives, and sex education. It
means having access to a health-care professional who provides sufficient information to help a patient make competent
decisions.

Most fundamentally, though, reproductive freedom means
assuring women and girls the power to control if and when

they will be mothers. When women lose control of these important decisions, there are significant repercussions in all areas of their lives: whether they will attend high school or college, the type of work they can seek, where they will live, whether they will be financially independent, and all the other important decisions that go into creating a fulfilling and rewarding life. Historically, when women have lacked such power, they have become, essentially, second-class citizens.

Access to comprehensive reproductive health care is essential to having control over your body. Without access to such care, you will not be able to have your health problems diagnosed, you will not receive education about how to avoid health-care problems, and you will not be able to obtain any necessary treatments.

Unfortunately, many women and girls in this country are unable to obtain appropriate health care. For many, lack of health insurance is the primary barrier. For others who live in remote rural areas, there may be a shortage of health-care providers and clinics equipped to deal with their health-care needs. And others simply do not know how to obtain health care in their communities.

Many people view this as a civil-rights problem to some extent: a lack of access often occurs when courts, Congress, and state legislatures place legal limits upon women's access to reproductive health care. These limits may take many forms, such as a denial of Medicaid funding for abortions for low-income women, or a failure to allocate money to conduct research about women's health-care needs.

This chapter looks at some of the most pertinent issues in this area, including contraception, abortion, and HIV/AIDS testing and treatment.

CONTRACEPTION

Many people believe that the right to freely make contraceptive choices is part of a woman or girl's larger constitutional right of privacy and liberty; they believe these decisions are basic to individual dignity and autonomy.

Abstinence and contraception are the only ways to prevent unwanted pregnancies. To be effective, both methods also require education: education about conception (when the sperm fertilizes the egg), one's body, methods of contraception (birth-control pills, IUDs, condoms, etc.), and the emotional, physical, and financial responsibilities that accompany child rearing. There are important reasons for education:

• From society's point of view, it is important that children be wanted. It is not in anyone's interests to bring children into the world who will not be loved and properly cared for.

• Pregnancy before a girl is emotionally or physically prepared can be harmful to her.

• Early pregnancies can result in children with severe health problems. Studies have shown that teenagers who become pregnant are less likely to obtain prenatal care—that is, sufficient medical attention during the pregnancy—than are adults.

Knowledge about birth-control methods and contraceptive availability (what kinds there are, and where they may be found) protects the health of the woman or girl. The problems posed by unwanted pregnancies, for both mother and child, have been so serious that most countries, including the United States, have signed a United Nations document called the "Convention on the Elimination of All Forms of Discrimination against Women." This document recognizes that deciding the number and spacing of children is a human right and includes the right to information, education, and services—services that should include all medically approved and appropriate methods of family planning, to ensure a voluntary and free choice.

Is it legal for minors to obtain contraception?

Yes. The right to decide the number and spacing of children has long been declared a legal right in the United States, although before 1965 a state could forbid the sale or use of contraceptives and could criminally punish those found in violation of such law. In 1977, in *Carey v. Population Services International*, the Supreme Court decided that a state law prohibiting contraception distribution to those under sixteen years of age violated their right to privacy.[1] The Court rejected the argument that denying access to contraception would reduce premarital sexual activity. Instead, the Court stated that it would aggravate the problem of unwanted pregnancy and venereal disease.

What methods of contraception are available?

There are many. Abstaining from sexual relations is the most obvious. For those who decide to become sexually active, there are nonpermanent methods, such as birth-control pills (oral contraceptives), cervical caps, spermicidal sponges, intrauterine devices (IUDs), diaphragms, and female and male condoms.

Another contraceptive method is sterilization, which is quite common but not reversible. Sterilization as a method has been abused over the years in this country, and some women, especially Puerto Rican women, Native American women, and African-American women, have been forcibly sterilized, or sterilized without their consent. This is illegal and is discussed later in this section.

The most recent contraceptive method is Norplant, which

takes the form of six match-size rubber capsules containing a chemical called progestin levonorgestrel. Using a local anesthetic, a trained clinician inserts the capsules just under the skin on the inside of a woman's arm. Once implanted, Norplant provides extremely effective continuous protection for five years, at which time it must be replaced. When a woman wishes to discontinue the method, she can return to her health-care provider, who will remove the implants under local anesthesia. The most common undesirable effect of Norplant is disruption of the menstrual cycle, and an increase in the number of bleeding days and spotting days per cycle. Additionally, some women report headaches, depression, nervousness, fatigue, dizziness and nausea. The user may find that the implants are slightly visible, and the initial procedure is expensive.

Can teenagers obtain contraception from public health clinics without their parents' consent?

Generally, yes. In one case, a federal appellate court held that parents could not require the state to inform them when their children sought contraception from a state-funded clinic. In that case, and others, judges have decided that the rights of parents to raise their children are not infringed when the state merely provides minors with an opportunity to exercise their own free choice.

Do other barriers exist that make it difficult for minors to obtain contraception?

Yes. One problem is that many teenagers have a difficult time obtaining information about contraception. While most schools provide some type of sex education, there are some parents who believe that sex education should occur only at home, not in the schools. They believe that parents have a right to raise their children according to their own religious and moral beliefs, which may prohibit the sharing of this type of information. However, there are those who believe that people taking this position ignore the reality that many teenagers *require* knowledge because they have sexual relationships, become pregnant, and/or catch fatal diseases, such as AIDS.

Another barrier arises from court decisions in which judges have required parental involvement when a minor seeks an abortion. So-called pro-life groups are using these decisions to press for mandatory parental involvement whenever minors seek not just abortions but also contraception.

Still another barrier comes from what are called "parental rights" laws, which many pro-life groups have been working to pass in the states. These laws declare that parents have the right to control the raising of their children to the extent that minors can be prevented from obtaining confidential medical services, including contraception, testing for sexually trans-mitted diseases, and sex education. As of the time this book went to print, no state had yet adopted such a law.

Is it legal for schools to teach sex education?

Yes. Sex-education programs have been around for most of this century. Courts have said that sex-education programs do not violate the Constitution just because parents may not like their children to receive information about sex. This idea is not new: in the past (as well as now) parents have objected, for example, to use of reading materials in schools that they believe are offensive, such as evolutionary theory. Nonethe-less, judges have decided that mere exposure to "offensive" ideas cannot be enough to make a sex-education program unconstitutional, or else every governmental program that offended anyone could be declared illegal. For a judge to decide that a sex-education program illegally prevents people from practicing their own religion, he or she would have to determine that the sex-education program essentially *forces* people to engage in religiously offensive practices. No court has done this because parents can always engage in home schooling or send their children to private schools.

Sex-education programs, which among other things teach about protection from sexually transmittable diseases such as HIV/AIDS, have also been defended as protecting the public health, whose importance outweighs any individual claims to religious freedom.

Can parents remove their children from sex-education programs?

Yes. Some courts have allowed parents to withdraw their children from a sex-education class when they argued that forced participation violates their rights to practice their religious beliefs free from state interference. However, parents do not have a right to dictate the curriculum at the public school where they have chosen to send their children.[2]

Can condoms be legally distributed in public schools?

No court has held that condom-distribution programs violate the Constitution, although several courts have examined the issue. And school systems across the country have implemented condom-distribution programs.

As one example, in 1991 the New York City board of education approved a condom-distribution program in the city's high schools. Teenagers were not required to obtain parental consent prior to obtaining condoms, and parents were not allowed to exclude their children from the program. However, teenagers were not required to participate in the program. Additionally, the program made provision for education and counseling so that it was not simply condom distribution but also health education.

51

In response, several parents and a school-board member sued the city, arguing that the program encouraged premarital sex, in violation of their religious beliefs and the right to raise one's children according to one's beliefs. The judge disagreed, responding that the parents were still free to care for and teach their children as they saw fit. The judge said that their dislike of the program was not a good enough reason to decide that it was unconstitutional. The court also pointed out that the program had the positive result of providing an opportunity for enhanced parental involvement in their children's lives, not a usurpation of their parental rights.

What are the arguments for and against condom distribution in public schools?

Concern about the spread of HIV/AIDS, especially among teenagers, who now constitute 20 percent of all those with AIDS, has prompted many to support condom distribution in the schools as the only practical way to promote what is called "safe sex." These proponents argue that some teenagers are going to ignore adults who believe teenagers should abstain from sex, and that those teenagers will still be sexually active despite the AIDS crisis. The only way to protect them is to teach them about how the HIV virus is transmitted, how it can be prevented, and to give them condoms if this will make it more likely that they will practice safe sex.

Others argue that these programs constitute acceptance of premarital sex. Further, they argue that AIDS-education programs have not been working very well, and that many teenagers continue to practice unsafe sex. Thus, they claim that the condom-distribution programs do not really promote the state's interest in protecting public health. Advocates of the programs feel that abolishing them seems like the old adage of biting off one's nose to spite one's face. What about those teenagers who have attended safe-sex programs, they say, and who now practice safe sex or have decided to abstain from premarital sex altogether?

Some people also maintain that such programs are unnecessary because teenagers are still free to get condoms at health clinics and private businesses. The problem with this argument is that some teenagers will not take the time, nor do they have the money, to go to health clinics or a store.

May a girl or woman be sterilized without her consent?

Absolutely not, although this has happened in the past at different times in this and the last century, especially to women of color. In some cases, doctors or nurses would submit documents authorizing the sterilization of their daughters to parents who could not read and did not know what it was they were signing. In other cases, state officials threatened women that they would discontinue their welfare payments unless they agreed to be sterilized.

In response to what eventually was recognized as an extremely serious problem, a federal agency—the Department of Health and Human Services—issued regulations establishing requirements for informed consent for all the sterilizations that were being paid for by the federal government. These regulations, which apply to both men and women, prohibit sterilization of anyone under 21, require a 30-day waiting period after written consent is given, and require counseling in the person's own language about the irreversibility of the procedure and its risks, benefits, and alternatives. A health administrator cannot obtain a girl or woman's consent while she is in labor, having an abortion, or under the influence of drugs or alcohol. The regulations also prohibit the use of federal money for sterilization of the mentally incompetent and institutionalized. A person cannot be asked to consent to sterilization as a condition for obtaining or continuing to receive welfare or other government benefits.

Despite these measures, studies show that some hospitals that receive federal money disregard the regulations. Hospitals that do not receive federal money are not required to follow them.

ABORTION

Before 1973, when the Supreme Court legalized abortion in *Roe v. Wade*, abortions were legal only in certain states: New York, Washington, Alaska, and Hawaii. Nonetheless, many women still obtained abortions. For every legal abortion performed, experts estimated that anywhere from 100 to 190 illegal abortions were performed each year.[3] Many of these illegal abortions were not performed by trained medical professionals, and women frequently became infected, were sterilized, and even died.

Low-income women and women of color—who constitute the majority of women seeking health services from public facilities—suffered the most when safe, legal abortions were not available. Before *Roe*, 49 percent of pregnancy-related deaths in New York were due to illegal abortions. Of these deaths, 50 percent of the women were African-American, and 44 percent were Puerto Rican.[4]

Then, in Texas, a woman who called herself Jane Roe (not her real name) challenged a state law that allowed abortion only "for the purpose of saving the life of the mother." Her lawsuit led to one of the most important, famous, and controversial decisions in the country. Justice Harry Blackmun, writing for the Supreme Court, said in *Roe v. Wade* that abortions may not be outrightly banned, and declared that women have a constitutional right to privacy. This decision was meant to ensure that all women have the right to choose when and if they will become mothers, and more generally to protect the right of women to make decisions affecting their bodies.

What did the Supreme Court decide in *Roe v. Wade*?

The Court said that a Texas law making it a crime to obtain an abortion except "by medical advice for the purpose of saving the life of the mother" violated the Constitution. The Court also said that states may not prohibit or interfere with a woman's right to an abortion, in consultation with her physician, during the first trimester (three months) of pregnancy. From then until viability (about the twenty-fourth to twenty-eighth week of pregnancy, when the fetus potentially could survive outside the womb), the state can establish medical regulations governing abortion only if they are necessary to protect the woman's health. After viability, the state can prohibit abortions except when necessary to protect the life or health of the woman.

The Court further said that there should be a balancing test between the interests of the woman, on the one hand, and the state's desire to protect the woman and the fetus, on the other. While women have a constitutional right to privacy, the Court acknowledged that the state has an interest in protecting the health of the woman—and therefore has a right to be concerned about the potential life of the fetus in the last trimester before birth.

Justice Blackmun wrote:

> *The right of privacy . . . is broad enough to encompass a woman's decision whether or not to terminate her pregnancy. The detriment that the State would impose upon the pregnant woman by denying this choice altogether is apparent. Specific and direct harm medically*

diagnosable even in early pregnancy may be involved. Maternity, or additional offspring, may force upon the woman a distressful life and future. Psychological harm may be imminent. Mental and physical health may be taxed by child care. There is also the distress, for all concerned, associated with the unwanted child, and there is the problem of bringing a child into a family already unable, psychologically and otherwise, to care for it. In other cases, as in this one, the additional difficulties and continuing stigma of unwed motherhood may be involved. All these are factors the woman and her responsible physician necessarily will consider in consultation.

Can women lose the rights secured by *Roe v. Wade*?

Yes. The Supreme Court can overrule a prior decision, which means that the Court can change its mind, as discussed in chapter 1. This rarely happens, however, because of the importance of precedents, also discussed in chapter 1—the prior decisions of other judges on cases that are very similar to the one being decided. Nonetheless, because there exists a very vocal group of people who oppose the right to choose whether to have an abortion, courts have been willing to chip away at the rights guaranteed in *Roe v. Wade*, and even to reconsider the decision itself.

As you may remember, there are nine justices who sit on the Supreme Court. Each has one vote. In order for one side of a dispute to win, it must be able to get five votes. Those justices who are part of the five (or more) are called the majority. Those who are not are called the dissenters.

Since the Supreme Court decided *Roe*, the composition of the Court has changed. President Ronald Reagan, who was elected in 1980, and President George Bush, who was elected in 1988, both appointed justices to the Court who are opposed to the right to choose an abortion. At the time of this writing, there are three justices on the Court—William Rehnquist, Antonin Scalia, and Clarence Thomas—who have stated that they want to overrule *Roe*. Two or more justices would create the majority needed to make abortion illegal again.

Thus, the rights guaranteed by *Roe* hang by a precarious thread. There have been a number of cases in recent years that demonstrate just how fragile the right is. In 1992, for example, the Supreme Court decided a case called *Planned Parenthood v. Casey*, which stopped short, by the narrowest of margins, of overruling *Roe*. Instead, however, the Court applied a new test to determine whether a state law prohibiting abortion is unconstitutional: whether the law has the "purpose" or "effect" of placing a "substantial obstacle in the path of a woman seeking an abortion before the fetus attains viability."

This test will encourage even more restrictions on the right to choose abortion free from government interference. Even so, Justice Blackmun, who wrote the court's opinion in *Roe v. Wade*, called the majority opinion, written by Justices O'Connor, Kennedy, and Souter, "an act of personal courage and constitutional principle." This is because these justices resisted the pressure by other justices, Antonin Scalia and Clarence Thomas in particular, to overrule *Roe*.

Can states make abortion illegal?

No. The Supreme Court decision in *Roe* is the law of the land. However, the Court has made it much more difficult for women to get abortions by allowing state legislatures to restrict access to the procedure. This is being done in a number of ways.

The Court has an opportunity, whenever a state enacts a law that restricts access to abortion, to overrule *Roe*, so long as someone challenges the constitutionality of the law. For example, in one recent case, *Webster v. Reproductive Health Services*, the Court decided that a state law prohibiting abortions in public facilities (such as health clinics that get government funding) or by public employees (those who work at such clinics) is constitutional.

The Court has also decided that states can require parental involvement before minors can obtain abortions (*Hodgson v. Minnesota* and *Ohio v. Akron Center for Reproductive Health*); that medical facilities receiving federal funding can be prevented from discussing with their patients whether abortion is even an option (*Rust v. Sullivan*); and that states can make women wait 24 hours, or that minors must obtain the consent of one parent or a judge, before they can get an abortion (*Casey*).

After *Webster*, 500 abortion restrictions and bans were introduced in state legislatures. Pro-choice forces were able to defeat the vast majority of these abortion-restriction efforts, although often by only the slimmest of margins. Those laws that have passed tend to fall into three categories: abortion bans, "roadblock" laws, and minors' laws. The minors' laws, perhaps the most popular new legislation, are discussed below in a separate section. Some of these laws include:

Bans: Louisiana and Guam currently prohibit all abortions as a matter of criminal law, with limited exceptions—if there is immediate danger to a woman's life and in certain cases of rape or incest. There are sometimes exceptions for fetal abnormalities and threats to a woman's health as well. Frequently, the exceptions are so vaguely worded that doctors cannot tell when an abortion would be illegal. Most fundamentally, however, these prohibitions would deprive virtually all women of their right to abortion, if passed by the remaining states and upheld by the Supreme Court.

Roadblocks: This approach does not seek to prohibit all abortions. Instead, it sets obstacles in a woman's path to free and informed decision making. Mississippi and North Dakota adopted this approach with new laws that establish a mandatory delay and require women to receive state-devised abortion information. Other roadblock techniques include mandatory spousal notification, state reporting requirements, and severe clinic-licensing requirements.

In some states, legislatures have created laws that require doctors to delay the performance of an abortion for 24 or 48 hours after the woman first gives her informed consent to the procedure. Delay laws often force women to travel twice to receive medical care, which can discourage some from returning and can provide anti-choice activists with time to seek these women out and harass them at their homes. These laws also direct doctors to give women specific information intended to discourage them from having the abortions—even if the information is irrelevant, unnecessary, or misleading. For example, in Wisconsin, the state assembly approved a bill that would require a woman seeking an abortion to meet with a physician to receive counseling, including an offer to view a sonogram of the fetus. In some situations the materials included descriptions of the fetus as well as information about agencies offering alternatives to abortion and child-support benefits.

Many people feel that these laws serve no legitimate state interest, arguing that these laws are not needed because women already take considerable time to make this decision of such obvious importance. They point out that state laws, as well as the standards of the medical profession, ensure that health-care practitioners provide women with accurate and unbiased information about their health-care options and also obtain women's informed consent to the procedures.

Some people also feel that these laws are dangerous to

women's health. Because there are no abortion providers in 83 percent of all United States counties, many women must travel long distances to obtain abortions. In Illinois, for example, 91 percent of all counties do not have anyone who can perform an abortion. In addition, most clinics schedule abortion procedures only one or two days a week. As a result, mandatory 24- or 48-hour waiting periods can result in two-week delays, necessitating more costly and medically risky abortions.

Does a minor have a right to obtain an abortion without notice to, or the consent of, one or both parents?

Only in the states that have not created parental-involvement laws. The following 35 states now have some kind of laws on the books that prevent minors from obtaining abortions without parental consent or notice, or that require mandatory counseling. But only the 25 states with asterisks were enforcing the laws as of August 1995.

Alabama*
Alaska
Arizona
Arkansas*
California
Colorado
Delaware*
Georgia*
Idaho
Illinois
Indiana*
Kansas*
Kentucky*
Louisiana*

Maryland*
Massachusetts*
Michigan*
Minnesota*
Mississippi*
Missouri*
Montana
Nebraska*
Nevada
New Mexico
North Dakota*
Ohio*
Pennsylvania*
Rhode Island*

South Carolina*

South Dakota

Tennessee*

Utah*

West Virginia*

Wisconsin*

Wyoming*

Do these state laws affect all women the same?

No. Efforts to limit abortion rights, while profoundly affecting all women, have the strongest impact on low-income women and women of color, who, as noted earlier, make up the majority of women seeking services from public facilities.

In the past, many women who could not afford abortions would go to medical facilities that receive money from the federal government. As discussed earlier in this chapter, now *Rust* allows interference with the speech of federally funded physicians, and *Webster* and *Casey* permit states to pass new laws under which women may be prohibited from obtaining abortions and abortion-related services in public hospitals (though not in private facilities). And a series of Supreme Court decisions have allowed the federal government and many state governments to eliminate Medicaid funds for abortion.

Must a woman obtain the consent of the fetus's father or notify him before getting an abortion?

No. The Supreme Court has ruled that states may not force a woman to obtain the father's consent for an abortion.[5] The Court reasoned that "inasmuch as it is the woman who physically bears the child and who is more directly and immediately affected by the pregnancy as between the two, the balance weighs in her favor."[6]

Many people oppose notificaiton and these consent requirements, saying that they force women to bear children against

61

their will and that they also are based on the assumption that women are unable to make important life decisions. Opponents also argued that they cause women physical harm: only women suffer the health effects of pregnancy.

These requirements, opponents point out, also reflect a double standard. The law has never required a father to notify his wife when he is making medical decisions that may affect his ability to bear children. Thus, a wife need not give her consent when her husband is sterilized, receives treatment for prostate cancer, or takes a drug that affects his ability to bear children.

Further, the vast majority of women who choose abortion voluntarily involve the men in their lives in their decision making. Women who do not may have very good reasons not to do so. For women in troubled or abusive marriages, for example, notification requirements do not foster better communication, the purported goal of such requirements. Rather, the laws enable husbands to force their wives sometimes, through physical violence or economic or psychological coercion, to carry an unwanted pregnancy to term.

For similar reasons, women are also not required to notify the fathers that they intend to obtain an abortion. Although the Court has not addressed the validity of husband or father "notification" requirements, many lower-court decisions have found that the reasoning of the "father consent" cases applies equally to cases dealing with notice.[7]

HIV/AIDS[8]

Young women today should be very concerned about Acquired Immune Deficiency Syndrome (AIDS). It is the fourth leading cause of death for all women; it is the second leading cause of death for African-American women; it is the third leading cause of death among Hispanic women.[9]

AIDS is a disease that can affect anyone: men and women, old people and young people, white people and people of color. Yet one difficulty facing women with HIV or AIDS, and women at risk of getting this disease, is that the medical community has tended to act as if AIDS is exclusively a man's disease. The result is that doctors are not always alert for its symptoms in girls or women, which can mean that it is diagnosed late, causing a delay in treatment and, sometimes, a faster death.

What are HIV and AIDS?

HIV is a virus that attacks the immune system. The healthy immune system fights off diseases and infections, but when it has the HIV virus it cannot protect the body efficiently. Eventually an HIV-afflicted immune system will be irreparably damaged, and diseases will take over. Even diseases that normally may not be life threatening become so to someone whose immune system is no longer functioning. Some diseases tend to be experienced more by women, blacks, hemophiliacs, and drug users, such as pulmonary tuberculosis, recurrent pneumonia, and invasive cervical cancer. Yeast infections can be a warning signal that someone may have the HIV virus; women and girls who experience frequent and severe yeast infections should get tested.

The definition of this disease changes as we learn more about it. For example, the Centers for Disease Control (CDC)— the principal governmental agency that monitors the frequency of the disease, establishes federal policies that affect access to health care, and funds critical research—defined the disease for a long time in such a way that many women who were HIV-infected, or actually had AIDS, were not diagnosed by doctors as having HIV. This happened because many of the types of infections that women with HIV get are not experienced by men and these infections were not identified as consistent with an HIV or AIDS diagnosis. The result was that many women could not get federal financial and medical assistance for their treatment. Under pressure from health-care and women's organizations, the CDC has changed the definition of the disease to include infections experienced by women.

How does someone get the HIV virus?

The two most common ways of transmission are through drug use by injection and sexual intercourse. (Current statistics indicate that women and girls are getting the HIV virus primarily through sexual intercourse.) Blood-based bodily fluids transmit the virus, which can be exchanged through oral contact or through anal or vaginal intercourse. Female-to-female transmission of HIV appears to be rare, although cases have been reported. Heterosexual transmission (women with men) is more common for both sexes in younger age groups. Condom use is extremely important to prevent transmission, even with someone you think does not have the virus.

Use of drugs, especially crack, greatly enhances the risk because drug users typically have more sex partners, and engage in unprotected sex more often.

How can someone find out if she or he has AIDS?

In 1985, a test was created to identify the presence of HIV that may be obtained at facilities generally called Ryan White Health Care Centers (although the exact names will vary). (Ryan White was a boy who died of AIDS.) Most doctor's offices offer the test. Home tests are now available, although there is some controversy as to how accurate they are. Planned Parenthood, which is a national organization with offices in most cities and states, also provides the tests or can help someone obtain a test.

Schools in 41 states are now required to teach about the HIV virus and AIDS. For example, schools in Maryland must provide annual instruction to all students at least once from third grade through high school.

May teenagers be subjected to HIV testing without their consent?

It depends.

As a matter of principle, testing should not be performed without your informed consent. This means that a medically trained person provides you with enough information about the risks associated with any drug or course of medical treatment so that you can make an educated decision about whether it is something that you want to have happen. For HIV testing, a medical person should also let you know what the test involves, what it means if you test positive, where you can get treatment, and if the results will be confidential.

As of 1990, at least 34 states had laws requiring that HIV testing not happen without informed consent.[10] In addition, a federal law (Ryan White CARE Act) contains a provision requiring states that receive federal money to develop informed-consent requirements for HIV testing.[11] More than half the states have passed laws that require a minor's consent for an HIV test or allow minors to consent to diagnosis and treatment of sexually transmitted or venereal disease without obtaining parental consent.[12]

In addition, there are now state laws that allow minors to consent to medical treatment if they are pregnant or homeless.

However, many teenagers never have the opportunity to make an informed decision about HIV testing. Many do not know where to go, or they may fear that medical personnel will disclose the results. Few places provide adequate counseling services for teenagers.[13] And there is a widespread lack of understanding about whether teenagers can give their own consent for an HIV test.

The issue of reproductive rights is a profound one, and it is at the heart of the struggle for equality for women. Margaret Sanger, a pioneer in the movement for birth control, once said: "No woman can call herself free who does not own and control her body. No woman can call herself free until she can choose consciously whether she will or will not be a mother." The AIDS crisis presents such a threat to human life that many girls will never survive to the age where they can make this decision. Education about how AIDS is transmitted, and sex education generally, has become necessary for survival.

5

YOUR HOME AND FAMILY

Relationships. That's all there really is. There's your relationship with the dust that just blew in your face, or with the person who just kicked you end over end. . . . You have to come to terms, to some kind of equilibrium, with those around you, those people who care for your environment.

—Leslie Marmon Silko, quoted in *The Third Woman*

For many women, men, and children, the most difficult legal issue they ever face is that of divorce. It can lead to severe emotional, financial, and legal problems. One spouse may take all the money out of the savings account, or threats may be made about who will get custody of the children. The loss of one income may push the parent with custody of the children into poverty. The financial issues involved in the breakup of marriages have special importance for women and their children because divorce often causes a severe decline in their standard of living. (One study in California reported that one year after legal divorce, men experienced a 42 percent increase in their standard of living, while women experienced a 73 percent decline.) For this reason, good legal protection is critical at the early stages of separation, and steps should be taken to ensure that the children are not the main ones to suffer when a marriage breaks down.

The law bestows great benefits on families, as compared to individuals simply living together. The way a family is legally defined has changed over recent decades, and there is now greater tolerance in the law for a definition that does not fit the traditional norm of two parents with children. Many of the issues that arise for those who merely live together are the same as for those who are married.

Nonetheless, the legal definition of *family* continues to have important financial consequences. For example, family members can automatically inherit property; nonfamily can inherit only by will. And only family members can sue on behalf of another family member who dies as a result of an accident.

THE DIVORCE PROCESS

Until the beginning of this century, it was very difficult for couples to divorce. There was tremendous social stigma attached to anyone who got a divorce, especially for women. A divorced woman was considered morally unfit. Society viewed her as a failure as wife and mother, and thus as a person.

Divorce also carried serious financial and emotional costs. For a woman to divorce meant that she would surrender all rights to property and custody of her children. The premise of marriage was that the wife and husband were legally and morally a single entity. As Sir William Blackstone, a famous eighteenth-century legal commentator, wrote:

By marriage, the husband and wife are one person in law: the very being of legal existence of the woman is suspended during the marriage, or at least is incorporated and consolidated into that of the husband; under whose wing, protection and cover, she performs everything.

Consequently, many women remained in difficult and abusive relationships. The process of obtaining a divorce was also hindered by legal requirements that one party be at fault. This often led to ugly charges of infidelity and adultery from one spouse to another, and where women deviated from the traditional expectations of motherhood, to charges that they were incompetent and unstable parents. Sometimes these various charges were true, but sometimes they were not.

In recent decades, divorce law has become more flexible and progressive, and divorce no longer carries the stigma it once did. In fact, divorces are now extremely common (indeed, some would say much too common). Recent efforts by some groups, however, would reimpose the fault requirements in divorce in an attempt to slow down the divorce rate and keep families together. But as history has shown, it has been primarily women, and their children, who have suffered when divorces were difficult to obtain.

What are grounds for divorce now?

State law governs divorce law, so the standards vary. Generally, most states have what is called a "no-fault" law. This type of law allows couples to obtain a divorce without showing that one or the other is at fault. Such laws tend to make it easier emotionally on all involved because they eliminate the need for finger pointing and blaming. If someone wants a no-fault divorce, she or he can say there are irreconcilable differences (which means the couple's problems just cannot be worked out), or incompatibility (which means about the same thing). In some states it is possible to obtain a divorce on grounds of adultery (one partner has an affair with someone else), extreme cruelty, drug or alcohol addiction, or one partner's imprisonment (which renders the marriage unworkable).

The law varies as well with respect to the way in which divorces can be obtained. In some states, judges can grant a divorce even if only one spouse seeks it. In other states, both spouses are required to agree. And in still other states, the courts are required to make their own decision after hearing from both sides. This is why it is important to obtain a lawyer, although legal help may not be necessary when there are no children or there is no property to be dealt with.

How does someone get a divorce?

As mentioned above, obtaining a divorce is relatively easy if there are no children or property involved. In some areas, the clerk's office in state courthouses may have forms that the partners can fill out. Bookstores also often carry forms that can be purchased; these may be appropriate in these circumstances only. Generally, however, it is important for each party to consult and obtain his or her *own* lawyer because their interests (in property division, child custody, etc.) may not be the same.

In some states, there is a requirement that there first be what is called a legal separation. Generally the partners must file papers in court asking to become legally separated. They can enter into an agreement that deals with many complicated issues such as child custody, visitation rights, alimony, or property division. Usually the couple must live apart for a certain amount of time before they are allowed to officially ask for a divorce. The law has been set up this way so as to try and make sure that couples really want the divorce; sometimes a dispute may lead one or both of the partners to think that they want a divorce, but this may change once the dispute is over.

It is unusual for there to be a divorce trial in a courtroom before a judge. Usually disputes related to divorce are settled outside of court, and the judge then only needs to approve the divorce. However, if a couple cannot come to an agreement on important issues, then there will be a trial in which each party must present evidence in support of her or his position. The judge then decides the contested issues. This process can become quite costly, and makes what is essentially a private dispute into one that is public, which many people hope to avoid. Nonetheless, litigation sometimes is the only way to get a fair settlement.

Another alternative is mediation. This is a fairly new process that became relatively common in the 1960s, and involves a third party, such as a retired judge or professional mediators, who help both sides work out a settlement. The difference between mediation and litigation is that the mediator cannot impose her or his decision upon the parties. In some states, mediation is required prior to any litigation; in others, mediation is required on certain issues, such as child custody; and in other states it is encouraged, but not required.

Mediation has both advantages and disadvantages. One advantage is that it is usually faster and less costly than litigation. It can also be more informal and less emotionally charged. It works best when the partners have approximately equal bargaining power. Problems arise when the partners do not have equal bargaining power, such as when one partner is physically abusing the other, or when one partner is earning an income and the other is not.

Studies of mediation have revealed that mediation usually works to the woman's disadvantage. One reason for this is that in most states the process is not regulated and there are no legal standards to follow. Women have more rights in divorce than they used to, but they do not necessarily benefit from these advances when they are using the mediation process. Also, many women have been financially dependent on their husbands, so their bargaining power is less. Mediation can also be more time-consuming if it fails and the parties have to go to court. This would also make it more costly as well.

CHILD CUSTODY AND SUPPORT

The question of who will gain custody of the children is probably the most painful and difficult issue for everyone in the family during a divorce. In the last century, courts would automatically give custody of the children to the fathers because they were part of the "property rights" of the man. Then for many years, judges followed the "tender years" doctrine, which presumed that women were better custodians for young children, up until the age of seven. Children—and especially boys—beyond the "tender years" were presumed to be better off with their fathers. Fathers could obtain custody of very young children only if they could show that the mother was "unfit."

These rules based upon stereotypes created many problems. Courtroom battles could get very nasty, as fathers tried to drag in as much dirt about the mothers as they could. It also was based on a double standard: if a woman did not fit the traditional idea of a "good wife" and was, for example, unfaithful, then she could be deemed "unfit," while the man could do the same without suffering any adverse consequences.

Today, the situation has improved, and judges are required to decide what is in the best interests of the child. A judge makes a decision by listening to the lawyers for both the mother and father, and, if the child is old enough, sometimes listening to the child's opinions as well.

One of the biggest problems today is that divorce often sends women, who tend to be the primary caretakers, and their children into poverty, as a result of the loss of the father's income. It is these women, and their children, who make up the bulk of the poor in this country. In about two-thirds of single-parent families, in which the mother cares for the children, the father contributes no support at all. And only half the mothers due child support received full payment. This problem is made worse by the fact that the government has not adequately enforced child-support orders. Child-support enforcement is thus a very important problem.

How does a judge decide who gets custody?

In several states, judges will award custody to the parent who has acted as the primary caretaker. In most families this results in the woman getting custody, but in families in which the father has played a greater role in child rearing, he has a greater chance of convincing a judge that he should have custody.

Sometimes the best-interests test can lead to unfair results. For example, a judge may decide that the parent who has more money is better able to care for the child. This usually puts women at a disadvantage because women, for a variety of reasons, tend to be poorer: they often have lower-paying jobs; have sacrificed career prospects to raise a family; or have financially supported their husbands through college or graduate school. Judges, who are called upon to decide these custody issues during the divorce process, sometimes give custody to a father who has remarried, when the mother has not, believing that a two-parent household will be better, especially if the new wife does not work outside the home. Women do get custody in most cases, but that is usually because most men do not contest it. One study has shown that when men do request it, they prevail over half the time.

Even though the way of determining who should get custody has become fairer, stereotyping persists and continues to affect judicial decisions about who can better provide for a child. The case of Jennifer Ireland, discussed in chapter 2, is a good example. In that case, a judge awarded custody to the father, even though he had never lived with the child, because Ms. Ireland had started attending the University of Michigan and had placed their daughter in day care while she was in class; the father's mother was available to care for her in her home. After Ms. Ireland appealed the trial court decision to a higher court, the order was reversed and the case had to start all over before a different judge. Nonetheless, the case sent fear into the hearts of many women across the country who work, or are in school, and are trying to create a better life for themselves and their children.

Can both parents share custody?

Yes. There are different arrangements. There is joint custody, in which the parents share responsibility for the children on a daily basis; and split custody, in which each parent alternates having sole custody. These arrangements generally mean that the children spend an equal amount of time with each parent. In several states, both types are allowed only if both parents agree. In some states, neither arrangement is allowed. And in some states, the judges prefer joint custody.

Parents considering joint or split custody should consider whether it is desirable for their child to move repeatedly, and whether equal access to both parents is important. A key issue is whether the parents are able to deal with each other amicably on a daily basis.

The amount of child support must be carefully negotiated in both these situations. Fathers sometimes argue that they should not have to pay support if they have the children half the time (though usually they have more than half the income) and in fact they often keep the children little more than they might in the traditional custody arrangement.

How are child-custody arrangements enforced?

It is extremely important that the parent seeking enforcement obtain what is called a child-custody order. Until there is a child-custody order, both parents are equally entitled to custody of their children. Thus, even if a father or mother has signed a written agreement to leave the children with the other parent, either one may still legally take them. If that is of concern, it is important to get a temporary custody order prior to the actual divorce. This is especially important if there is a chance that one parent will move the children out of the state; without an actual court order ensuring custody for both parents, one parent may obtain a court order from another state that could be difficult for the other parent to challenge.

What does child support include?

Child support is usually established according to a formula set out in guidelines that the federal government has required the states to create. The guidelines cover essential items, such as food, clothing, and shelter. However, where a judge determines that applying the guidelines would be unfair or unjust then he or she is not required to comply with them.

Even though these guidelines exist, child-support awards still often fail to account for many of the expenses that exist in raising children. To be adequate, child support should include, where appropriate, money to go toward health insurance, or to pay medical expenses where health insurance does not cover such expenses. Common examples include bills for dentistry, glasses, and psychiatry. Some people feel that extras such as summer camp, travel, music or dance lessons, and college education should also be included.

Federal legislation requires periodic review of state guidelines. It also requires that individual support be awarded as necessary to make up for the increased cost of housing, groceries, and other essentials. It has been suggested that, to make things easier, separation agreements or court orders should provide for both an automatic cost-of-living adjustment and increased payments as children grow older and have higher expenses.

Who is entitled to child support?

The person (usually one of the parents) who has been given primary custody of the children. A woman can obtain child support even if she was not married to the father so long as she can establish paternity. This means that she can prove who is the father of the child; this may be accomplished through a blood test of the father and child. State agencies who have the responsibility for enforcing child-support orders will establish paternity as part of the enforcement process.

How are child-support orders enforced?

A federal law requires that child support be automatically withheld from paychecks unless both parties agree to an alternative arrangement or the judge finds that there is a good reason to establish one. The automatic-withholding method is not effective, however, for men who are self-employed or get paid for work in cash.

If the father has fallen behind on child-support payments, the mother has several options: she can hire a lawyer and file a lawsuit; she can go to her state or local child-support enforcement agency, which is usually part of the state social-services department, family court, probation office, or state's attorney general's office.

One problem with enforcement has been that for many years, cases languished at each stage of the process—stages such as establishing paternity, locating the father, and obtaining and enforcing child-support orders. A 1990 federal law (the Family Support Act) established certain time frames that states must follow, and this has improved the situation.

PROPERTY AND ALIMONY

A related issue is the question of who gets what in a divorce proceeding. As discussed earlier in this chapter, divorce still places many women at a significant financial disadvantage. Many women who marry young do not get enough training or education before marriage to maximize their wage-earning capacity. They may believe that their husbands will take care of them for the rest of their lives and that they need not plan for a career. Women's predominant role in rearing children further decreases their wage-earning capacity; even when a woman has managed to acquire education or training, she loses work experience during the years of child rearing.

Nor are women paid for their years of work in the home, even though such work is as important and valuable as employment outside the home. Some women work to put their husbands through professional or training school or other extended education without receiving the opportunity for comparable training themselves. As we have seen, most often it is the woman who takes custody of the children upon divorce. With these factors combined, alimony is often necessary to compensate women for these financial disabilities.

What is alimony?

Alimony, also called maintenance or spousal support, consists of periodic support payments to the husband or wife after the marriage has ended. It is designed to provide financial support for the financially dependent former spouse. These payments usually continue until the spouse receiving alimony remarries or until the alimony-providing spouse dies, although some states have rehabilitative alimony, which is designed to help a spouse in establishing herself in a job or furthering her education.

It is possible for a wife to return to court to ask for increased alimony if circumstances change or for the husband to ask for decreased payments if his income declines. Some states sharply limit the availability of alimony, depending on the length of the marriage; the wife's ability to earn money; the financial resources of the party requesting alimony; the time necessary for that person to acquire education or training for employment; the standard of living during the marriage; the age, physical fitness, and emotional condition of the party requesting support; and the ability of the other partner to meet his or her own needs and still contribute to the former spouse's support. Either spouse may be awarded alimony or child support.

How does a judge decide who gets what?

At the time of divorce, the property is divided between the husband and wife by separation agreement, property settlement, or court order. Each state has its own laws that govern the way it is done. Once a court decision has been reached, it is not usually possible to return later and ask that the question of property division be reopened.

Property includes all physical and financial possessions that have been acquired in the family after marriage up to the time of the divorce: cash, house, furnishings, car, boat, land, stocks, bonds, businesses, business interests, and so on. Pension rights are usually included, as is the value of a professional education or professional practice (such as legal or medical).

The basic rule is that jointly owned property may be evenly divided by the husband and wife. Some states have a rule that requires all community property be divided into two equal shares. Community property is all property acquired during the marriage; it does not include property owned prior to the marriage, property acquired during the marriage by gift or inheritance to one partner, or property acquired during the marriage that can be traced back to property included in one of those two categories. There are eight community property states: Arizona, California, Idaho, Louisiana, Nevada, New Mexico, Texas, and Washington.

Other states have rules based on the common law, under which marital property is not assumed to belong to both parties at the time of acquisition. In most common-law states, marital property must be "equitably divided" at the time of divorce. This principle can work differently depending on the state. The majority of states automatically exclude gifts and inheritances from consideration from either of these methods. Most courts consider a number of factors in making a decision about property. These include the length of the marriage; the age, health, and earning ability of husband and wife; and the contribution of each to homemaking and care of children, as well as their contribution in money or work to acquiring the property.

How can property and alimony disputes be avoided?

One way to avoid many problems is for spouses to enter into what are called premarital or marital agreements. A premarital agreement is a contract entered into before marriage that sets out the rights and obligations of both parties in the event of a separation or divorce. A marital agreement is a similar contract entered into during a marriage. Common issues include division of property, division of insurance and pension benefits, support of spouse at separation or divorce, provisions in a will, and child support for any children the couple may have while married. A premarital or marital agreement may not waive child support for any children the couple may have while married. The right to child support belongs to the child, not the parents.

Traditionally, premarital agreements were used by wealthy people to clarify financial arrangements and to protect property rights for their children or other relatives in the event of a divorce or the spouse's death. The wealthier partner in a couple where there is a large financial disparity may often insist upon such an agreement. They are sometimes used if one partner has children from a previous marriage. A wife who plans to support the relationship by being a full-time homemaker could also use an agreement, embodied in a document, to contract for an appropriate value of her services that recognizes the value of those services; courts may not protect her by ordering that she receive income based on an equal-partnership model at the time of divorce.

Premarital agreements can either harm or help women. A wealthy man can use one to attempt to ensure that a wife without assets will not get her fair share in a divorce. Conversely, the same wife could use one to attempt to ensure that she does get her fair share in a divorce. As these circumstances suggest, it is important to consider premarital and marital agreements very closely before signing them. It is advisable that each party retain a lawyer.

6

YOUR JOB

"Never doubt that a small group of thoughtful, committed people can change the world. Indeed, it is the only thing that ever has."

—Margaret Mead

Despite many advances, women continue to suffer discrimination when they look for jobs, seek raises or promotions, or even when they are simply trying to do their work. Discrimination in employment can take many forms: it may mean that a woman does not get hired for a construction job because of outmoded stereotypes that women cannot do heavy lifting; it may mean that a woman is fired because she is pregnant; it may mean that a woman is demoted because of her age; and it may mean that a woman has to suffer unwanted sexual advances at her place of employment.

One of the biggest problems is that women in greater proportion tend to find themselves in lower-paying professions. Also, women sometimes are paid less than men who are doing the same job. These are the primary reasons for what is now called the "feminization of poverty." This means that women are disproportionately represented among the nation's poor. As well-known feminist Susan Faludi writes in her book *Backlash*:

> *The already huge proportion of working women holding down menial clerical jobs climbed to nearly 40 percent by the early 80's, higher than it had been in 1970. By the late 80's, the proportion of women consigned to traditionally female service industries had grown too. A long list of "female" jobs became more female-dominated, including salesclerking, cleaning services, food preparation, and secretarial, administrative and reception work.*

It took a law called the 1964 Civil Rights Act (or Title VII, as it is commonly called), and a number of individual, courageous women fighting for their rights, to significantly improve the status of women in the workforce. This law requires that an employer may not discriminate against women, or against pregnant women. It applies to labor unions, employers, and employment agencies. It also protects teachers, those who work for state and local governments, and those who work for Congress. An employer must have at least fifteen employees to be covered by this law. The only exception is the United States government, which is not covered in the same way as other employers. Congress has amended this law several times since it was created, each time making it a little stronger.

Additionally, most states have passed one or more laws that forbid employment discrimination. The federal and state laws cover much the same practices, although state laws are often interpreted more conservatively. Still, in some cases, state laws provide greater protection by, for example, not limiting the amount of money a victim of discrimination may receive.

What is illegal employment discrimination?

There are a number of practices that used to be common but are no longer legal. These practices were based primarily on the assumption that women were the "weaker" sex, or that women would not want to work long hours or at night, or that women's proper place was in the home, and not in the workplace.

Based upon these stereotypes, state legislatures passed what were called "protective" labor laws at the turn of the century. These laws forbade women from working in certain jobs, working a certain number of hours, or doing certain kinds of work before or after childbirth. The federal courts eventually began ordering companies to stop using these laws to discriminate against women workers. Today an employer must give women the opportunity to show that they are qualified for a job involving physical strength; similarly, an employer may not refuse to hire women on the assumption that they could not meet the physical requirements of a specific job.

Another problem was that companies would sometimes force women to retire earlier than men. Sometimes, they gave women an option to retire earlier, to the disadvantage of men who wanted to leave earlier. And sometimes these companies allowed men to retire at the same age as women but with a lower pension than the women were given.

Pension benefits are the money that retired workers receive after working for a certain amount of time at a company, after they have left that job. In a landmark case in 1978, it was revealed that the Los Angeles Department of Water and Power took more money from their women workers than they did from men for the same pension benefits when they retired.

As a result, women had lower take-home pay than men. The department justified this discrimination by citing the statistic that women, on average, live longer than men. The Supreme Court declared this practice illegal because it prejudges and penalizes any woman who does not fit the average. The Court also said that it was illegal to give women lower monthly pension benefits than men.

Another example of job discrimination is the practice of paying women less than men for the same work. This happens because some people believe that women are not the primary breadwinners in a family and thus do not need the money as much. The practice was declared illegal when Congress enacted the Equal Pay Act (EPA) in 1963, which forbids employers from paying women who are doing the same work as men less than they pay those men.

In order for the EPA to apply, both men and women must work in the same place; the job of each must require equal skills, equal effort, and equal responsibility; the work must be performed under similar working conditions, and the tasks involved must be substantially the same. Examples include nurse's aides and orderlies in hospitals; assembly line workers in factories; janitors and maids; and salesclerks, no matter what kind of merchandise they sell.

Sex discrimination was an especially difficult problem for women workers who became pregnant. Many women who worked in the 1950s or 1960s were forced to quit their jobs when they became pregnant. Thanks to the Pregnancy Discrimination Act, enacted by Congress in 1978, discrimination based on pregnancy, childbirth, and related medical conditions is now illegal. This law requires that pregnant women who are able to work must be treated like other able workers, and that women disabled by pregnancy, childbirth, or related medical conditions must be treated like other disabled workers.

The rationale is that pregnancy is like other medical conditions: if a woman is physically incapable of working, just as a person with a broken leg may be incapable of working, she does not have to be kept on the job. But if she is physically able to work, an employer has no right to fire her. Moreover, even if she is temporarily unable to do part of her job, she still may have a right to transfer to another job—if that is how the employer treats other employees who are temporarily disabled from doing part of their job.

Thus, employers may not refuse to hire or promote a woman because she is pregnant, and may not question a female job applicant about her prior pregnancies, child care arrangements, marital status, and other such concerns if they do not make similar inquiries of male applicants.

Many other practices are illegal, and it would take a lengthy discussion to enumerate them all. Briefly, employers may not:

• refuse to hire or assign women of childbearing age to jobs where they will be exposed to substances or procedures that are allegedly hazardous to fetuses

• hire men and women for separate departments

• refuse to hire or promote women who are mothers because of their child care responsibilities if the company hires or promotes men who are fathers

• fire or refuse to hire women who have had abortions

• place help-wanted ads in sex-segregated newspaper columns, or seek only men or women for a particular position

• refuse to hire women because the company does not want to build a women's rest room

• establish different retirement ages or benefits for men and women

• give women fewer health-care benefits than men even if it costs more to provide some kinds of insurance to women than to men, such as coverage for pregnancy-related medical care.

What caused the gender-related laws to change?

One of the most important reasons these laws changed was because a few women took it upon themselves to argue not only on their own behalf, but also on behalf of all women in their position.

By definition, sex discrimination affects large numbers of women—whether they be 50 women in a small company, 50,000 women working at a large corporation, or the millions of women workers nationwide. To illustrate, if an employer refuses to promote Ann Smith because she is a woman, that employer is really saying that all women in Ann's position are ineligible for promotion.

This is an important concept for two reasons. First of all, understanding this point means that Ann's efforts should attack not only the particular decision not to promote her, but also the general policy that fails to promote women. Failure to do this, when appropriate, means that when another woman complains, the whole legal process must be repeated.

Second, it is far more difficult to prove discrimination against a particular woman than discrimination against many women. Companies can always find specific reasons for not promoting Ann Smith—she was frequently late to work, for example. When the employer must give reasons for a failure to promote all women, the excuses are harder to manufacture.

Does sex discrimination in employment continue today?

Yes. One problem that persists is sex segregation of jobs and the discrimination in pay that accompanies such segregation. For many years, feminists focused on getting equal pay for equal work. Even though this has been an important issue, it is not the real problem: most women do not do the work most men do.

The jobs dominated by women tend to be lower paying

than jobs involving comparable skills held by men—secretarial work, for example, as compared to construction work—and so women in the traditionally female professions get paid less.

A second problem is that even though *overt* discrimination has largely disappeared, more subtle forms of discrimination persist. Discrimination may exist even if the employer does not *intend* to discriminate.

An example of such a policy is the decision of a large company to upgrade the educational level of its workers by hiring only college graduates. This appears to be fair because it seems to apply equally to everyone. But until very recently more men received college educations than women. And the percentage of whites with college educations far exceeds the percentage of African-Americans. Thus, the *effect* of the policy is to exclude a disproportionate number of women and African-Americans from jobs with that company. And it may not be even necessary to have a college education in order to do a particular job in that company.

Another example is height and weight requirements. In one 1977 Supreme Court case, *Dothard v. Rawlinson,* a prison required that all guards be at least five feet two inches tall, and weigh a minimum of 120 pounds. Over 41 percent of all women could meet this standard, but 99 percent of all men were eligible. The Court ruled that the requirement discriminated against women because the impact fell more harshly on women, and then rejected the defense that the requirement was needed in order to hire strong guards. If strength is required, the Court stated, employers should directly test for strength, rather than rely on an inexact, unfair rule.

Since this decision, many other courts have invalidated height and weight rules, especially for police jobs.

Sexual harassment on the job is another pervasive problem that continues to harm women workers, and it is discussed later in this chapter. Additionally, in some circumstances, employers can refuse to hire pregnant women if the employer has a legitimate, nondiscriminatory reason for doing so. One court, for example, allowed a county court to withdraw an offer of a position as a staff attorney to a woman who disclosed her pregnancy after she had been offered the position. The court reasoned that it would be a bad business practice to hire a worker who would need to take a leave of absence during on-the-job training.

Employers may discriminate by altering a woman's conditions of employment after learning of her pregnancy. In such cases, the employer typically claims that the woman is not performing her job at an acceptable level. Courts usually decide these cases by examining evidence as to whether or not the employer's proffered explanation is "pretextual," which means that an employer is using a false reason as a cover-up for its real decision to terminate, demote, or otherwise discriminate against a pregnant woman because of her pregnancy.

Can employers ever limit jobs to either men or women?

Rarely. In general, an employer who wants to exclude all men or all women from a particular type of job must show two things: (1) that the job duties that the one sex cannot perform are essential to the functioning of the business, and (2) that members of the excluded sex cannot perform those job duties or that it is impossible to make individual determinations as to whether that person can perform those job duties.

One example of a circumstance in which an employer was allowed to exclude all women was for the position of guard in a maximum-security prison in Alabama. In 1977 the Supreme Court considered that the prison had a "jungle atmosphere" with sex offenders throughout the population, and decided that in this setting, women guards would be vulnerable to sexual

assault and unable to maintain order. Some employers have
been successful in excluding women or men when they argued
that there are unique concerns for modesty or privacy. These
include jobs as washroom attendants or certain kinds of nurses.

Can women be paid less than men for the same or similar work?

No, although this was once a widespread problem. In the 1960s
and 1970s, many women began to demand equal pay for equal
work, and the first major federal legislation outlawing pay discrimination, the Equal Pay Act, embodied this concept. To
establish that women are not getting equal pay for equal work,
it must be shown that there are men workers who perform
work that is substantially the same as the work performed by
women, and that both work in the same place. Only if all conditions are present does the employer have to increase female
wages to the level of male wages.

There is an even bigger problem: women and men are segregated into very different or unequal kinds of work. In 1987,
for example, women held 1.5 percent of the 3 million jobs in
the United States construction industry.[1] And according to
1994 data, only 10.5 percent of all dentists are female while
99.3 percent of all dental hygienists are female; although
women comprise 23 percent of all attorneys, among law-firm
partners—who earn the highest salaries—they make up only
10 percent. As of 1991, women constituted 82 percent of the
total administrative workforce.[2] Thus, a demand for equal pay
is virtually futile. Since workers are segregated by sex in this
country, women must switch their focus from equal pay to inte-
gration of jobs and to increasing the wage level of "female"
jobs. The problem that remains is how to prove that particular
women's jobs are worth the same as the more highly paid
men's jobs and that some portion of a wage differential is due

to sex discrimination. Lawyers use several methods—job evaluation studies and statistical analysis—which are sometimes successful.

Can pregnant workers get special benefits not available to men?

The Pregnancy Discrimination Act, a federal law, does not allow employers to provide special benefits to pregnant workers on the theory that laws treating pregnant women differently from other workers will eventually be used against women, as they have been in the past. Instead, women disabled by pregnancy-related conditions are entitled to any benefits that men obtain, such as the same sick leave and sick leave pay and benefits that a man might get for a broken leg, the same health insurance payments, and the same amount of time off.

Yet states are free to enact their own laws. A few states, such as California, Connecticut, Massachusetts, and Montana, allow employers to treat pregnant women more favorably than other employees with temporary illnesses. In 1977, in *California Federal Savings and Loan Association v. Guerra*, the Supreme Court upheld a California law that required employers to provide women disabled by pregnancy, childbirth, or related medical conditions with up to four months' unpaid disability leave for the length of their disability. They then had the right to return to the same or a similar job in the company. The Court ruled that in enacting the Pregnancy Discrimination Act, Congress provided "a floor beneath which pregnancy disability related benefits may not drop—not a ceiling above which they may not rise." However, the Court added, special treatment may not be based on archaic or stereotypical generalizations about the abilities of pregnant workers. And special treatment is limited to the period of time that a woman is actually disabled.

Are employers required to pay for health insurance benefits for abortions?

Not unless the woman's life would be endangered if the pregnancy were continued until term, or unless there are special complications requiring additional medical care.

What is sexual harassment?

This is a complex situation, but generally it includes unwanted sexual advances, employment decisions based upon acceptance or rejection of sexual favors, and offensive remarks or pictures in the workplace that interfere with an individual's work performance. It is a serious problem, especially for women entering jobs usually held by men. When these kinds of conditions exist, an employer can be found guilty of sexual harassment. Sexual harassment violates Title VII of the 1964 Civil Rights Act.

What steps can a woman take to protect herself against sexual harassment?

First, a women must say no in very clear terms. If the first refusal does not stop the problem, then she must inform management in writing and ask them to take steps to end it. A lawyer should be consulted at the earliest stage. Copies of all correspondence should be kept, along with detailed notes about any conversations, which include date, time, names, and as many details as possible. These documents will become very important later on if the situation comes down to the victim's word against her harasser's, or if the company tries to deny knowledge of the problem. If a woman decides to file charges, she needs to do so as soon as possible.

It is difficult to prove sexual harassment in court. Documenting someone's behavior can be hard. Also, there are some judges who are very unsympathetic to women claiming harassment; they may feel that it is not inappropriate for men to be sexually aggressive in the workplace, and that women often invite such behavior by being flirtatious. It is hard to challenge such prejudices as these.

Can an employer be legally held responsible for sexual harassment even if he or she was unaware it was happening?

If an employer fires an employee for refusing his sexual advances, then yes, the company could be found responsible. But the answer is not as clear-cut in the case of sexual harassment by co-workers, customers, or clients. An employer could be held liable, but only if the employer knew or should have known what was going on.

How can an employee prove that she or he has been discriminated against on the basis of gender?

There are many different ways to attempt to prove such a claim. One of the most important, and most successful, is through the use of statistics. For instance, even though a company may hire a lot of women, it would be significant if statistics reveal that women hold only 1 percent of the managerial or highly paid blue-collar jobs and 95 percent of the lower-paying secretarial jobs. Additionally, it may have to be shown that women are present in the labor pool of blue-collar or managerial workers, but are not hired for those jobs in proportion to their availability.

A second way to prove discrimination is through company documents, which sometimes set forth clearly illegal practices. The pension plan booklet may reveal that men and women must or may retire at different ages, solely because of their gender. The health-care plan may show that pregnancy is not covered or is covered only minimally, although full coverage is provided for all other medical conditions. The collective-bargaining agreement (the agreement that includes various benefits agreed to by unions and employers) may use female pronouns for certain jobs, male pronouns for others—clearly indicating that the company reserves some jobs for women and some for men.

A third way to prove discrimination is through the testimony of company workers and officials. Co-workers may be willing to testify about discriminatory statements they may have heard (for example, if a manager told them he would never hire a woman for a particular job because it is not suitable for women), or that they knew of the existence of a discriminatory job practice, or that the company's claim that women do different work from men is untrue.

What remedies can judges give to victims of discrimination?

In cases of intentional discrimination, Title VII allows victims of discrimination to get both punitive awards (designed to financially punish the perpetrators) and compensatory awards (designed to compensate for monetary losses).

Judges can also order an employer to stop the discriminating practice; to enforce rules prohibiting that practice; to provide money for the pain suffered by the victim; to pay the victim's costs in filing the lawsuit, lawyer's fees, backpay, and so on. The judge can also order a company to recruit and hire more women, to transfer them to better jobs, to train them for different positions, to change discriminatory health plans, and to increase women's wages.

What steps should someone take who believes she is experiencing discrimination at work?

It makes sense to approach the employer to discuss the problem, and to give the employer an opportunity to correct the problem prior to the filing of a lawsuit. If such a strategy does not seem advisable, either because it is fairly clear that the employer will not change the problem, or because alerting the employer may make it harder to collect evidence, then a lawsuit may be necessary.

Lists of employment-discrimination experts can be obtained from the local Equal Employment Opportunity office. A woman may be asked to pay the lawyer on a contingent-fee basis. This means that the lawyer will take his or her fee from a portion of the victim's awards in the case.

DECLARATION OF SENTIMENTS AND RESOLUTIONS

When, in the course of human events it becomes necessary for one portion of the family of man to assume among the people of the earth a position different from that which they have hitherto occupied, but one to which the laws of nature and of nature's God entitle them, a decent respect to the opinions of mankind requires that they should declare the causes that impel them to such a course.

We hold these truths to be self-evident; that all men and women are created equal; that they are endowed by their Creator with certain inalienable rights; that among these are life, liberty, and the pursuit of happiness; that to secure these rights governments are instituted, deriving their just powers from the consent of the governed. Whenever any form of government becomes destructive of these ends, it is the right of those who suffer from it to refuse allegiance to it, and to insist upon the institution of a new government, laying its foundation on such principles, and organizing its powers in such form, as to them shall seem most likely to effect their safety and happiness. Prudence, indeed, will dictate that governments long established should not be changed for light and transient causes; and accordingly all experience hath shown that mankind are more disposed to suffer, while evils are sufferable, than to right themselves by abolishing the forms to which they were accustomed. But when a long train of abuses and usurpations, pursuing invariably the same object, evinces a design to reduce them under absolute despotism, it is their duty to throw off such government, and to provide new guards for their future security. Such has been the patient sufferance of the women under this government and such is now the necessity which constrains them to demand the equal station to which they are entitled.

The history of mankind is a history of repeated injuries and usurpations on the part of man toward woman, having in direct object the establishment of an absolute tyranny over her. To prove this, let facts be submitted to a candid world.

He has never permitted her to exercise her inalienable right to the elective franchise.

He has compelled her to submit to laws, in the formation of which she had no voice.

He has withheld from her rights which are given to the most ignorant and degraded men—both natives and foreigners.

Having deprived her of this first right of a citizen, the elective franchise, thereby leaving her without representation in the halls of legislation, he has oppressed her on all sides.

He has made her, if married, in the eye of the law, civilly dead.

He has taken from her all right in property, even to the wages she earns.

He has made her, morally, an irresponsible being, as she

can commit many crimes with impunity, provided they be done in the presence of her husband. In the covenant of marriage, she is compelled to promise obedience to her husband, he becoming to all intents and purposes, her master—the law giving him power to deprive her of her liberty, and to administer chastisement.

He has so framed the laws of divorce, as to what shall be the proper causes, and in case of separation, to whom the guardianship of the children shall be given, as to be wholly regardless of the happiness of women—the law, in all cases, going upon the false supposition of the supremacy of man, and giving all power into his hands.

After depriving her of all rights as a married woman, if single, and the owner of property, he has taxed her to support a government which recognizes her only when her property can be made profitable to it.

He has monopolized nearly all the profitable employments, and from those she is permitted to follow, she receives but a scanty remuneration. He closes against her all the avenues to wealth and distinction which he considers most honorable to himself. As a teacher of theology, medicine, or law, she is not known.

He has denied her the facilities for obtaining a thorough education, all colleges being closed against her.

He allows her in Church, as well as State, but a subordinate position, claiming Apostolic authority for her exclusion from the ministry, and, with some exceptions, from any public participation in the affairs of the Church.

He has created a false public sentiment by giving to the world a different code of morals for men and women, by which moral delinquencies which exclude women from society, are not only tolerated, but deemed of little account in man.

He has usurped the prerogative of Jehovah himself, claiming it as his right to assign for her a sphere of action, when that belongs to her conscience and to her God.

He has endeavored, in every way that he could, to destroy her confidence in her own powers, to lessen her self-respect, and to make her willing to lead a dependent and abject life.

Now, in view of this entire disfranchisement of one-half the people of this country, their social and religious degradation— in view of the unjust laws above mentioned, and because women do feel themselves aggrieved, oppressed, and fraudulently deprived of their most sacred rights, we insist that they have immediate admission to all the rights and privileges which belong to them as citizens of the United States.

In entering upon the great work before us, we anticipate no small amount of misconception, misrepresentation, and ridicule; but we shall use every instrumentality within our power to effect our object. We shall employ agents, circulate tracts, petition the State and National legislatures, and endeavor to enlist the pulpit and the press in our behalf. We hope this Convention will be followed by a series of Conventions embracing every part of the country.

RESOLUTIONS

Whereas, the greater precept of nature is conceded to be, that "man shall pursue his own true and substantial happiness." Blackstone in his Commentaries remarks, that his law of Nature being coeval with mankind, and dictated by God himself, is of course superior in obligation to any other. It is binding over all the globe, in all countries and at all times; no human laws are of any validity if contrary to this, and such of them are as valid, derive all their force, and all their validity, and all their authority, mediately and immediately, from this original; therefore,

Resolved, That such laws as conflict, in any way, with the true and substantial happiness of woman, are contrary to the great precept of nature and of no validity, for this is "superior in obligation to any other."

Resolved, That all laws which prevent woman from occupying such a station in society as her conscience shall dictate, or which place her in a position inferior to that of man, are contrary to the great precept of nature, and therefore of no force or authority.

Resolved, That woman is man's equal—was intended to be so by the Creator, and the highest good of the race demands that she should be recognized as such.

Resolved, That the women of this country ought to be enlightened in regard to the laws under which they live, that they may no longer publish their degradation by declaring themselves satisfied with their present position, nor their ignorance, by asserting that they have all the rights they want.

Resolved, That inasmuch as man, while claiming for himself intellectual superiority, does accord to woman moral superiority, it is preeminently his duty to encourage her to speak and teach, as she has an opportunity, in all religious assemblies.

Resolved, That the same amount of virtue, delicacy, and refinement of behavior that is required of woman in the social state, should also be required of man, and the same transgressions should be visited with equal severity on both man and woman.

Resolved, That the objection of indelicacy and impropriety, which is so often brought against woman when she addresses a public audience, comes with a very ill-grace from those who encourage, by their attendance, her appearance on the stage, in the concert, or in feats of the circus.

Resolved, That woman has too long rested satisfied in the circumscribed limits which corrupt customs and a perverted application of the scriptures have marked out for her, and that it is time she should move to the enlarged sphere which her great Creator has assigned her.

Resolved, That it is the duty of the women of this country to secure to themselves their sacred right to the elective franchise.

Resolved, That the equality of human rights results necessarily from the fact of the identity of the race in capabilities and responsibilities.

Resolved, *therefore*, That, being invested by the Creator with the same capabilities, and the same consciousness of responsibility for their exercise, it is demonstrably the right and duty of woman, equally with man, to promote every righteous cause by every righteous means; and especially in regard to the great subjects of morals and religion, it is self evidently her right to participate with her brother in teaching them, both in private and in public, by writing and by speaking, by any instrumentalities proper to be used, and in any assemblies proper to held; and this being a self-evident truth growing out the divinely implated principles of human nature, any custom or authority adverse to it, whether modern or wearing the hoary sanction of antiquity, is to be regarded as a self-evident falsehood, and at war with mankind.

Resolved, That the speedy success of our cause depends upon the zealous and untiring efforts of both men and women, for the overthrow of the monopoly of the pulpit, and for the securing to woman an equal participation with men in the various trades, professions, and commerce.

Seneca Falls, N.Y., 1848

NOTES

Decisions of the federal courts are contained in multivolume
sets of books known as the Federal Supplement (abbreviated
"F.Supp.") for the district courts, the Federal Reporter (abbreviated "F.," "F.2d.," or "F.3d") for the courts of appeals, and
United States Reports (abbreviated "U.S.") or Supreme Court
Reports (abbreviated "S.Ct.") for the Supreme Court. The names
of the parties involved in the case come first, next the volume
number, next the name of the reporter, next the page on which
the case begins, next the name of the court, and finally the date
of the decision. For example, 376 F.Supp. 750 (M.D.Fla. 1974)
means that the case appears in volume 376 of the Federal Supplement on page 750 and was decided by the district court for
the middle district of Florida in 1974. The librarian at a law
school or a library that has law books can help you locate any
of the decisions that are cited in this book. The decisions are
also available online through Westlaw and Lexis, and through
the World Wide Web.

CHAPTER 1

1. *Bradwell v. The State*, 83 U.S. (16 Wall. 130) (1873).

2. Henry M. Lyman, M.D., et al., *The Practical Family Doctor: 20th Century Household Medical Guide*, 1891.

CHAPTER 2

1. Kary Moss, "Standardized Tests as a Tool of Exclusion: Improper Use of the SAT in New York," *4 Berkeley Women's L.J. 230* (1989–90).

2. Brief for Petitioner, at 2, *Franklin v. Gwinnett County Public School District*, 503 U.S. 60 (1992).

3. *Franklin v. Gwinnett County Public School District*, 503 U.S. 60 (1992).

4. *Faulkner v. Jones*, 51 F.3d 440 (4th Cir.), 116 S.Ct. 352 (1995).

5. 497 U.S. 417 (1990).

6. *Ireland v. Smith*, 214 Mich. App. 235, 542 N.W.2d 344 (Ct. App. 1995), aff'd, modified, 451 Mich. 457, 547 N.W.2d 686 (1996).

7. 8 N.Y.C.R.R. § 135.4(c)(7)(ii)(c)(2).

8. *Lantz v. Ambach*, 620 F. Supp. 663, 665 (S.D.N.Y. 1985) (citing attorney general's brief at 19).

9. *Id.* at 665, quoting *Mississippi University for Women v. Hogan*, 458 U.S. 718, 725 (1982).

10. Stephen Labaton, "Benefits Are Refused More Often to Disabled Blacks," *The New York Times*, May 11, 1992, at 1.

11. *Kirchberg v. Feenstra*, 450 U.S. 455 (1981).

12. *Wengler v. Druggists Mut. Ins. Co.*, 446 U.S. 142 (1980).

13. *Stanton v. Stanton*, 421 U.S. 7 (1975) and 429 U.S. 501 (1977).

14. *Craig v. Boren*, 429 U.S. 190 (1976).

15. See, for example, *Rostker v. Goldberg*, 453 U.S. 57 (1981) (upholding federal law providing that men but not women must register for the draft); *M. v. Superior Court of Sonoma County*, 450 U.S. 464 (1981) (upholding California statutory rape law making boys and men but not girls or women criminally liable for consensual sex with an opposite-sex partner who is under the age of eighteen); *Geduldig v. Aiello*, 417 U.S. 484 (1974) (upholding California law providing workers' disability benefits to all disabled men, but not to women workers disabled by childbirth).

16. *Rostker v. Goldberg*, 453 U.S. 57 (1981).

17. *Feeney v. Personnel Administration of Massachusetts*, 445 U.S. 901 (1980).

18. *Commonwealth v. PIAA*, 18 Pa. Commw. Ct. 45, 334 A.2d 839 (1975).

19. 3 C.F.R. 339 (1964–65 Comp.); 3 C.F.R. 684 (1966–70 Comp.).

20. 29 U.S.C. 621 (1996); 29 C.F.R. pt. 1625.

CHAPTER 3

1. E. Flexner, *Century of Struggle*, 29–30 and n. 13 (1970).

2. *Kirstein v. Rector and Visitors of University of Virginia*, 309 F. Supp. 184 (E.D. Va. 1970).

3. 20 U.S.C. §1681 (1996).

4. 42 U.S.C. §295h-9 (1996); 42 U.S.C. 298b-2 (1996).

5. 20 U.S.C. §2301 (1996).

6. 42 U.S.C. §2301 (1996).

7. 20 U.S.C. §1701 (1996).

8. *Mississippi University for Women v. Hogan*, 458 U.S. 718 (1982).

9. *Newberg v. Board of Public Education*, 330 Pa. Super. 65, 478 A.2d 1352 (Pa. Super 1984).

10. *Garret v. Board of Education of School District,* 775 F. Supp. 1004 (E.D. Mich. 1991).

11. *See Mississippi University for Women v. Hogan,* 458 U.S. 718, 738–9 (1982) (Powell, dissenting).

12. *Sanchez v. Brown,* C.A. No. 69-C-1615 (E.D.N.Y. 1971).

13. 34 C.F.R. 106.34(e).

14. 34 C.F.R. 106.36.

15. Cal. Educ. Code 9246 (West 1973).

16. See "Sex Discrimination: The Textbook Case," *62 Cal. L. Rev. 1312* (1974) for a discussion of the effects of textbook stereotypes and the efforts to eliminate biased books in California, Pennsylvania, and Kalamazoo, Michigan.

17. 34 C.F.R 106.40.

18. *Romans v. Crenshaw,* 354 F. Supp. 868 (S.D. Tex. 1971); *Holt v. Shelton,* 341 F. Supp. 821 (M.D. Tenn. 1972); *Davis v. Meek,* 344 F. Supp. 298 (N.D. Ohio 1972).

19. *Pfeifer v. Marion Center Area School District,* 700 F. Supp. 269 (W.D. Pa. 1988); *But see Wort v. Vierling,* 778 F.2d 1233 (7th Cir. 1985).

20. 20 U.S.C. 1681(a) (6), (7) and (8) (1996).

21. *See Brenden v. Independent School District,* 477 F.2d 1292 (8th Cir. 1973); *Bednar v. Nebraska School Athletic Association,* 531 F.2d 922 (8th Cir. 1976); *Clinton v. Nagy,* 411 F. Supp. 1396 (N.D. Ohio 1974).

22. *Haffer v. Temple University of Commonwealth System of Higher Education,* 678 F. Supp. 517 (E.D. Pa. 1987).

CHAPTER 4

1. *Carey v. Population Services International,* 431 U.S. 678 (1977).

2. *See Brown v. Hot, Sexy and Safer Productions, Inc.*, 68 F.3d 525 (1st Cir. 1995).

3. Marian Faux, *Roe v. Wade: The Untold Story of the Landmark Supreme Court Decision That Made Abortion Legal* (1988), 11.

4. *See generally* Nsiah-Jefferson, "Reproductive Law, Women of Color, and Low-Income Women," in *Reproductive Laws for the 1990s*, 17–58 (N. Taub and S. Cohen, eds. 1988).

5. *Planned Parenthood v. Danforth*, 428 U.S. 52, 67–72 (1976).

6. *Id.*

7. *Conn v. Conn*, 525 N.E. 2d 612 (Ind. Ct. App.)(husbands intervention rejected); *Coleman v. Coleman*, 57 Md. App. 755, 471 A.2d 1115 (1984)(same).

8. The author would like to thank Abigail English, Catherine Teare, and the Youth Law Center for their assistance with this section.

9. Centers for Disease Control and Prevention (CDC), "Update: Mortality Attributable to HIV Infection Among Persons Aged 25–44 Years—United States, 1991 and 1992," *Morbidity and Mortality Weekly Report* 42 (1993): 869–72.

10. David A. Hansell, "HIV Antibody Testing: Public Health Issues," in *AIDS Practice Manual*, ed. Albert et al., 3–5.

11. 42 U.S.C. § 300 ff. 61(b)(1) (1996).

12. Abigail English, "Adolescents and HIV: Legal and Ethical Questions," in *The HIV Challenge*, ed. Marcia Quackenbush and Kay Clark, 2nd ed. (Santa Cruz, CA: Network Publications, 1995), 259–85; Abigail English, "Expanding Access to HIV Services for Adolescents: Legal and Ethical Issues," in *Adolescents and AIDS: A Generation in Jeopardy*, ed. Ralph J. DiClemente (Newbury Park, CA: Sage Publications, 1992), 265–66.

13. English, "Expanding Access," 266–67.

14. Abigail English, "AIDS Testing and Epidemiology for Youth: Recommendations of the Work Group on Testing and Epidemiology," *Journal of Adolescent Health Care* 10 (1989): 52S.

CHAPTER 6

1. C. Udell, *Signaling a New Direction in Gender Classification Scrutiny, United States v. Virginia*, 29 *Connecticut Law Review* 521, 560 (1996).

2. Law, "Girls Can't Be Plumbers: Affirmative Action for Women in Construction: Beyond the Goals and Quotas," *24 Harv. C.R.-C.L.L. Rev. 49*, 50 (1989).

RESOURCES

For Further Reading

Biographies

Atkinson, Linda. *Mother Jones: The Most Dangerous Woman in America*. New York: Crown, 1978.

Bataille, Gretchen. *Native American Women: A Biographical Dictionary*. New York: Garland, 1993.

Boyd, Melba Joyce. *Discarded Legacy: Politics and Poetics in the Life of Frances E.W. Harper, 1825–1911*. Detroit, Mich.: Wayne State University Press, 1994.

Davidson, Sue. *A Heart in Politics: Jeannette Rankin and Patsy Mink*. Seattle, Wash.: Seal Press, 1994.

Foner, Philip Sheldon. *Three Who Dared: Prudence Crandall, Margaret Douglass, Myrtilla Miner: Champions of Antebellum Black Education*. Westport, Conn.: Greenwood Press, 1984.

Goodsell, Willystine. *Pioneers of Women's Education in*

the United States: Emma Willard, Catherine Beecher, Mary Lyon. New York: AMS Press, 1970.

Haskins, James. *Barbara Jordan.* New York: The Dial Press, 1977.

Jackson, George. *Black Women Makers of History: A Portrait.* Distributed by National Women's History Project, 1975.

McLenighan, Valjean. *Women Who Dared.* Milwaukee, Wis.: Raintree, 1979.

Meyer-Rolka, Gail. *100 Women Who Shaped World History.* San Francisco, Calif.: Bluewood Books, 1994.

Painter, Nell Irvin. *Sojourner Truth: A Life, a Symbol.* W. W. Norton: New York, 1996.

Palmer, Alice Mulcahey. *Alice Freeman Palmer: Pioneer College President.* Englewood Cliffs, N.J.: Prentice-Hall, 1970.

Peavy, Linda, and Ursula Smith. *Women Who Changed Things: Nine Lives That Made a Difference.* New York: Scribner's Sons, 1983.

Runyon, Randolph. *Delia Webster and the Underground Railroad.* Lexington, Ky." University Press of Kentucky, 1996.

Shields, Barbara. *Women and the Nobel Prize.* Minneapolis, Minn.: Dillon Press, 1985.

Sickels, Eleanor. *Twelve Daughters of Democracy: True Stories of American Women, 1865–1930.* New York: Viking Press, 1996.

Education

AAUW Educational Foundation. *How Schools Shortchange Girls: The AAUW Report: A Study of Major Findings on Girls and Education.* Washington, DC: National Education Association, 1992.

Hammer, Trudy. *The Gender Gap in Schools: Girls Losing Out.* Hillside, N.J.: Enslow, 1996.

Weis, Lois, and Michelle Fine, Eds. *Beyond Silenced Voices: Class, Race and Gender in United States Schools*. Albany, N.Y.: State University of New York Press, 1993.

Employment

Colman, Penny. *Rosie the Riveter: Women Working on the Home Front in World War II*. New York: Crown, 1995.

Glazer, Perina M., and Miriam Slater. *Unequal Colleagues: The Entrance of Women into the Professions, 1890–1940*. New Brunswick, N.J.: Rutgers University Press, 1987.

Sokoloff, Natalie J. *Black Women and White Women in the Professions: Occupational Segregation by Race and Gender, 1960–1980*. New York: Routledge, 1992.

Lesbian and Gay Rights

McCaulsin, Mark. *Lesbian and Gay Rights*. New York: Crestwood House, 1992.

Penelope, Julie. *Out of the Class Closet: Lesbians Speak*. Freedom, Calif.: 1994.

Sex Discrimination

Hammer, Trudy. *Sexism and Sex Discrimination*. Danbury, Conn.: Franklin Watts, 1990.

Sexual Harassment

Gay, Kathlyn. *Rights and Respect: What You Need to Know about Gender Bias and Sexual Harassment*. New York: Marshall Cavendish, 1994.

Hodgson, Harriet W. *Powerplays: How Teens Can Pull the*

Plug on Sexual Harassment. Minneapolis, Minn.: Deaconess Press, 1993.

Kutner, Lawrence. "With a 1990's Awareness of Sexual Harassment, Grownups Look at 'Harmless' School Bus Teasing." *The New York Times*, national edition (February 24, 1994): B5.

LeBlanc, Adrian Nicole. "Harassment at School: The Truth Is Out." *Seventeen* (May 1993) 134–135

Slavery

Morton, Patricia. *Discovering the Women in Slavery: Emancipating Perspectives on the American Past*, Atlanta, Ga.: University of Georgia Press, 1996.

Yee, Shirley J. *Black Women Abolitionists: A Study in Activism, 1828–1860.* Knoxville, Tenn.: University of Tennessee Press, 1992.

Sports

Helmer, Diana Star. *Belles of the Ballpark.* Brookfield, Conn.: Millbrook Press, 1993.

Macy, Sue. *A Whole New Ball Game: The Story of the All-American Girls Professional Baseball League.* New York: Henry Holt, 1993.

Suffrage

Sullivan, George. *The Day the Women Got the Vote: A Photo History of the Women's Rights Movement.* New York: Scholastic, Inc., 1994.

Teenagers

Gravelle, Karen. *Soaring Spirits: Conversations with Native American Teens*. Danbury, Conn.: Franklin Watts, 1995.

Kaklin, Susan. *Speaking Out: Teenagers on Race, Sex and Identity*. New York: G.P. Putnam Sons, 1993.

Women's Movement

Archer, Jules. *Breaking Barriers: The Feminist Revolution from Susan B. Anthony to Margaret Sanger to Betty Friedan*. New York: Viking Press, 1991.

Ash, Maureen. *Cornerstones of Freedom: The Story of the Women's Movement*. Chicago: Chicago Press, 1989.

Flexner, Eleanor. *Century of Struggle: The Women's Rights Movement in the United States*. New York: Antheneum, 1973.

Johnston, Norma. *Remember the Ladies: The First Women's Rights Convention*. New York: Scholastic, Inc., 1995.

Women's Rights

Foner, Philip S. *Frederick Douglas on Women's Rights*. Wesport, Conn: Greenwood Press, 1976.

Schneir, Miriam, Ed. *Feminism: The Essential Historical Writings*. New York: Vintage Books, 1972.

Wollstonecraft, Mary. *Vindication of the Rights of Women*. New York: Alfred A. Knopf. 1992.

ORGANIZATIONS

American Civil Liberties Union
Children's Rights Project
404 Park Avenue South, 11th Floor
New York, NY 10016
(212) 683-2210

    The Children's Rights project brings lawsuits behalf of children in the child-welfare system to improve the quality of care that they receive.

American Civil Liberties Union
Women's Rights Project
132 W. 43rd Street
New York, NY 10036
(212) 549-2500

    The ACLU Women's Rights Project has brought major litigation protecting the rights of women, particularly in the areas of employment discrimination, child support, and health care.

Center for Reproductive Law and Policy
120 Wall Street, 18th Floor
New York, NY 10005
(212) 514-5534

    The CRLP works to ensure that all women have access to safe and affordable reproductive health care. Its focus is on young women, low-income women, rural women, and women of color, whose reproductive health care needs have been largely neglected.

Children's Defense Fund
25 E. Street, NW
Washington, DC 20001
(202) 628-8787

Exists to provide a strong and effective voice for all children in America who cannot vote, lobby, or speak for themselves. It pays particular attention to the needs of poor, minority, and disabled children. The CDF's goal is to educate the nation about the needs of children and encourage preventive investment in children before they get sick, drop out of school, suffer critical family problems, or get into trouble. Provides information and advocacy in many areas, including health care, child abuse, violence, and child care.

Children's Rights of America hotline
(800) 442-4673

Advocates for missing and abused children and runs a 24-hour hotline to help youths in crisis.

Child Welfare League of America
440 First Street NW
Suite 310
Washington, DC 20001-2085
(202) 638-2952

National organization of 775 public and private child welfare agencies.

National Abortion Rights Action League
1156 15th Street NW
Washington, DC 20005
(202) 973-3000

NARAL works to protect the reproductive rights of women and promote adequate reproductive health care.

National Center for Youth Law
114 Sansome Street, Suite 900
San Francisco, CA 94104-3820
(415) 543-3307

This organization seeks to improve the lives of poor children and youth. Through legal advocacy, NCYL has confronted issues that adversely affect American's poor children for more than two decades. These issues include child abuse and neglect, foster care quality and standards, and the health of children and adolescents. The NCYL has special expertise in AIDS-related issues for adolescents.

National Coalition of Advocates for Students
100 Boyleston, Street, Suite 737
Boston, MA 02116
(617) 357-8507

Umbrella organization of local student advocacy groups. Provides information about special education, corporate punishment, misclassification, etc.

National Information Center for Children and Youth
with Disabilities
P.O. Box 1492
Washington, DC 20013-1492
(800) 695-0285

An information clearinghouse that provides information on disabilities and disability-related issues. Children and youth with disabilities (birth to age 22) are the special focus.

National Organization for Women
1000 16th Street NW
Washington, DC 20036
(202) 331-0066

Has convened three summits for young feminists; its most recent was held in 1997 in Washington, DC. Many local chapters have young feminist task forces or committees working on issues pertaining to young women's rights, including condom distribution in schools, sex education, etc.

NOW Legal Defense and Education Fund
99 Hudson Street
New York, NY 10013
(212) 925-6635

Provides a legal resource kit for women's rights.

National Women's Law Center
1616 P Street NW
Washington, DC 20036
(202) 328-5160

Women's rights organization that addresses broad range of issues including health and reproductive rights, family support, child care, employment, and education.

Youth Advocacy Center
281 Sixth Avenue
New York, NY 10014
(212) 675-6181

Runs a twelve-week training program in advocacy skills for teenagers in foster care to negotiate conflicts in foster care and confront challenges.

INDEX

A

Abortion, 45, 54–62, 85

  denial of Medicaid funding for, 46, 61

  health insurance benefits, 91

  illegal, 54

  notification of fetus's father, 61–62

  parental consent requirement for minors, 5, 20–21, 50, 58, 60

  privacy rights and, 30

  right to, 19

  roadblock laws, 59–60

  Roe v. Wade, 5, 54–57

  Supreme Court decisions, 5, 20–21

Acquired Immune Deficiency Syndrome (AIDS), *see* HIV/AIDS

African-Americans, 87

  equal-protection clause of Fourteenth Amendment and, 27

  HIV/AIDS among female, 62–63

  illegal abortions and, 54

  slavery of, 3, 23

  subtle discrimination against, 15

C

Index